PRAYING
WITH A
PASSIONATE
HEART

PRAYING WITH A PASSIONATE HEART

Bridget Mary Meehan
and
Regina Madonna Oliver

Liguori
LIGUORI, MISSOURI

Published by Liguori Publications
Liguori, Missouri
http://www.liguori.org

Library of Congress Cataloging-in-Publication Data

Meehan, Bridget.
   Praying with a passionate heart / Bridget Mary Meehan and Regina Madonna Oliver. — 1st ed.
     p. cm.
   ISBN 0-7648-0212-7
   1. Prayer—Christianity. I. Oliver, Regina Madonna, 1931– . II. Title.
BV210.2.M43 1999
248.3'2—dc21   98–35989

Printed in the United States of America
03 02 01 00 99 6 5 4 3 2

DEDICATION

To my parents, Jack and Bridie Meehan; Aunt Molly McCarthy; my brothers, Patrick and Sean; my sisters-in-law, Valerie and Nancy; my niece and nephew, Katie and Danny.

—Bridget

To my parents, Harvey and Ethel Oliver; Aunt Fran Webster; my brother David and sister-in-law Diane Oliver; my nieces and nephews David Michael and Ellen Oliver, James Webster and Sylvia Ho Oliver, Barbara and Mark Forth, and Carol Lee Oliver Tuohey; my niece Laura Anne Forth and nephew William Webster Oliver; my cousins Eleanor Lamb and Edy Jo and Melissa Southard.

—Regina

To our friends and mentors: Irene Marshall, Mary and Joe Beben, Charlie Davis, Sr. Mary Cashman C.D.P., Sr. Patricia Ann Carroll S.C.N., Sandra and Kevin Voelker, Francis Keefe, John Weyand, Joe Mulqueen, Eileen Dohn, Marcia Tibbits, Betty Wade, Rea and Tom Howarth, Patricia Byrne, Kathleen Bulger, Patricia McAleavy, Richard Sforza, Homer Sabatini, Andree Lanser, Daisy and Ogden Sullivan, Peg and Bob Bowen, Rosemary Walsh, Jim and Patty Burch, Donna Mogan, Ginny Koenig, Joni and Michelle Whalen, Luz and Rafael Sandiego, Doug and Jojo Sandiego, Michal Morches, Maria and Steve Billick, Ginger Avvenire, Mary and Kevin Fitzgibbons, Megan Fitzgibbons, Consilia Karli, Maureen Miele, Nancy Healy, Susan and Gerald Gordon, Sara Muenster, Mary Trail, John Adams, Paul Imse, Sharon Freeman, Sr. Rita McGarvey, Fr.

Joseph McGarvey, Fr. Ron Falotico, Louis Benoit, Sr. Josefita Marie I.H.M., Kay and David Welsh, Pat Lehrer, Virginia Limon, Doris and Bob Schlesinger, Virgil and Darlene Spurlock, Robert Hampson, Carol Ann Williams, A. J. and Lisa and Aaron Jarvis, Gavina and Alexis King, Fr. Edward McCorkell O.C.S.O., Fr. Paul Wynants, C.I.C.M., Kathy Kopac, Kay Graf, Mary Ambrosia, Kaye Brown, Peggy Gott, Ann Tennison, Eileen Thomas, Ken Knapp, Pat Zimmerman, Jim Webster, Mary Jean Kane, Rochelle Applewhite, Fr. David Kessinger O.S.B., Sally Ann Nelson, Phyllis Kessinger, Phyllis and Wendell Hurst, Olga Gane, Charles Gane, Nancy Forbes, Estelle Spachman, Mary Pauls, Kay Brown, and Katherine Nee. Also Sisters for Christian Community; the Graduate Theological Foundation of Donaldson, Indiana; The Catholic University of America; Virginia Theological Seminary; Washington Theological Union; Shalem Spiritual Institute, Washington, D.C.; and Spalding University, Louisville, Kentucky (formerly Nazareth College) and Marquette University.

To Anthony Chiffolo, editor at Liguori, with gratitude.

Contents

INTRODUCTION

Have you ever longed for something more in life? Do you sometimes feel overwhelmed with unpaid bills, cranky children, a demanding career, a messy house, aging, the loss of family members through death or divorce, health problems, not enough time to even think about everything you have to accomplish before the end of the day…stress, stress, stress? Welcome to the human race! You are not alone. The good news is that you can experience the infinite, boundless love of God for you, no matter how insane you think your life is. If you look around you, help is on the way. Grace is everywhere. God is right beside you. As the prominent theologian Karl Rahner reminds us, God is always already there.

Every person is a living, breathing, praying person. Every moment, every feeling, thought, desire, and action of our lives can reveal God's abiding presence. All we have to do is become aware of this wondrous love. In other words, we can pray always because God is forever loving us every moment of every day of our lives. We can choose to invite God to share with us the good times, the hard times, the times we feel like dancing with angels, the times we are in the pits of darkness and pain. To pray with a passionate heart means learning to feel, think, and experience with our whole being all that life is. It means using our imagination, feelings, and thoughts to open ourselves to the divine touch in our souls.

A woman who came for spiritual guidance said that she could not pray because worry and fear had become a way of life for her: "I am always wondering, 'What if this happens? what if that happens?' Sometimes I'm a nervous wreck and am too overwhelmed to pray." Yet Jesus tells us to come when we are heavily burdened. In the gospels Jesus reminds us not to be anxious or afraid. "Peace I leave with you, my peace I give you. Don't let your hearts be distressed; don't be fearful" (John 14:27 *Inclusive New Testament*). These are words that challenge us to let go of fear and trust in God's tremendous love. If you sometimes feel like this woman, you can take comfort because Jesus loves you in the midst of your concerns. All you have to do is come as you are to Jesus and "let it all hang out." No need to rehearse a nice speech. No need for special language. Simply give it to Jesus in whatever way you can. Pour out your feelings honestly to the Healer of your heart. Jesus will embrace and hold you close. When this happens, you'll experience unfathomable love as Jesus frees you from useless anxiety and gives you peace. Jesus will assure you: "I know how you feel—love, joy, hurt, worry, pain—you can bring it all to me."

Medieval mystic Mechtilde of Magdeburg visions a God who tenderly wraps divinity's arms around us and sings us a love song: "O lovely rose on the thorn! O hovering bee in the honey! O pure dove in your being! O glorious sun in your setting! O full moon in your course! From you, I, your God, will never turn away."*

---

*Sue Woodruff, *Meditations with Mechtilde of Magdeburg*, Santa Fe: Bear & Company, 1982, 34–35.

Like Mechtilde, we too can fall in love with God. We can join hands and hearts with people from every race, religion, and ethnic group around the globe. Then our walls of separation and division will fall down. We will talk and laugh, sing and dance, work and play together at last. We will discover that bliss flows out from us because the reign of God is within us (Luke 17:21). In other words, we can be a family who delights in God and one another, as we pray with passionate hearts.

Saint Augustine once reflected, "The love with which we love God and love one another is the same love." A priest friend, Father John, often listened for hours to people talk about their troubles. He taught people much about pastoral ministry just by the way he cared for people. They came flocking to his door at all times of the day and night. He welcomed them warmly and made them feel as if they did him a favor. His coworkers sometimes grew concerned that he might miss an important meeting or be late for Mass, but this beloved priest never even wore a watch: he was always there for people. He spoke to their hearts with his understanding. He had a tremendous gift for bringing calm and tranquility to the most tortured lives. Some called him the "Shepherd of the Broken Wings." Father John heard people's pain at the deepest level of his being and touched their wounds with the compassion of Christ. Basking in this love, people seemed to open like roses to the warm sun. He simply lived his life making the love of God and love of neighbor the most important thing of all. Isn't that what the gospel is all about? As the First Letter of John tells us, "Beloved, let us love one another because love is of God; everyone who loves is begotten of God" (1

John 4:7 *Inclusive New Testament*). When we love like this, we are praying with a passionate heart.

Skeptics may say that this is a naïve expectation in today's real world. Some think it is the impossible dream. But if not we who are baptized into Christ, then who? If not now, then when? Others may question, "But how can this happen?" In people like John we see the reality lived out.

The sage tells us that every important journey begins with a first step. The first step is the solitude of prayer when we journey to the center of our being. Here we can experience the compassion of God for all humanity. The God who is love expands our hearts. In God's presence we enter into the hearts of our sisters and brothers everywhere and realize that this is where God prays in us. Here we can become one with them on a profoundly spiritual level. Here we can listen to their longings, be aware of their pains, share their feelings, walk with them in their struggles, and imagine a new world transformed in love and justice. Here we can experience the dream of Jesus. Here we can drown in the infinite depths of Divine Love. Here we can become one in the heart of our God. We can listen to God assure us that we are loved, experience deep love with another, live joyfully and peacefully each day, share our feelings with God, bless the messes, forgive and let go, celebrate the Spirit's empowerment, expect God to talk to us, listen to the Holy One in the events and relationships of our lives, and discover womenspirit rising in our consciousness as we share with soul sisters. We can let go of fear as we live in the presence of divinity, experiencing grace joyfully uniting us with everyone and everything.

It is our hope that the readers of this book will sink into

amazing, wondrous grace as they contemplate God's bound-less love in every area of their lives. Each moment is an opportunity to experience blessings, revitalizing, strengthening, healing, renewing, and nurturing us. God's goodness is forever present. Life is gift. All is gift! No matter what happens, in the end, "All shall be well, and all shall be well, and all manner of things shall be well…" (Julian of Norwich). Let us walk together in communion with all creation on this most beautiful pathway of God's love, and as Teresa of Avila, Doctor of the Church, reminds us, "Let nothing disturb you, let nothing affright you. All things are passing. Only God is changeless. Who has God wants for nothing. God alone suffices." Then we pray with a passionate heart!

Pastoral ministry of listening is prayer. opening to the whole of humanity x listening.

PRAYING
WITH A
PASSIONATE
HEART

1
EXPERIENCE DEEP LOVE
WITH ANOTHER

Bridget

On September 25, 1996, my parents celebrated their golden wedding anniversary. Our family and friends gathered around the table, praised God for Mom and Dad's fifty years, celebrated a liturgy and renewal of marriage vows, and shared a delicious outdoor picnic. Then we sang and danced late into the evening to Irish songs and tunes from the forties. But the most wonderful memory for me was watching Dad and Mom sitting close together, holding hands and smiling at each other with a warmth of love that lit up the evening sky. In the midst of this party everyone's eyes were drawn upward to the pinnacle of our roof as granddaughter Katie pointed with a breathless "Oh, look!" to two doves nestling together. We could feel God's presence embracing us all.

When we encounter the depths of love, we enter the presence of God. One of the most beautiful gifts of life is to experience this kind of spiritual presence. As we love another, we discover the beauty of God's love within us, joining our hearts in a spiritual communion. In our relationships we learn to listen to one another and share our ideas, feelings, and dreams. We learn to experience the world through another human being's perspective. The experience of intimacy with another energizes and strengthens us to meet life's greatest challenges.

Holocaust survivor and author Victor Frankl credits his survival to the spiritual presence he maintained with his wife during his imprisonment. This relationship sustained him throughout the darkest days of his life.

"As my friend and I stumbled on for miles, slipping on icy spots, supporting each other time and time again, dragging one another up and onward, nothing was said but we both knew: Each of us was thinking of his wife. Occasionally I looked at the sky, where the stars were fading and the pink light of the morning was beginning to spread behind a dark bank of clouds. But my mind clung to my wife's image imagining it with an uncanny acuteness. I heard her answering me, as with her smile and frank and encouraging look. Real or not, her look was then more luminous than the sun which was beginning to rise" (*Man's Search for Meaning*).

One way to experience this spirit-to-spirit connection with others is by initiating a prayerful dialogue with them. We can do this with people who are present and wish to participate in this encounter. For example, couples who have made marriage encounters deepen their relationship by writing love letters to each other on a regular basis. I'll never forget the marriage encounter weekend that Regina, my coauthor, and I made at the urging of a priest-chaplain to enhance our ministry as counselors and planners of marriage-preparation and -enrichment programs. Regina and I strengthened our friendship that weekend through our sharing. I was touched by the strong and honest feelings the team expressed about their successes and failures to love as married couples. But I was deeply moved by the open communication that occurred. It was apparent that some painful issues emerged as couples shared their feelings about their relationships, acting as "living sacraments" to each other: healing, nurturing, challenging, and loving. "Love is a decision," the marriage encounter motto, means that every day, married couples have an opportunity to be lovers in every aspect of their lives, from the time they get up in the morning to the time they retire at night. Married love reflects the passionate, boundless love in the heart of God inviting human beings everywhere into caring relationships with others. God is love and embraces us through other persons. In other words, each of us needs other people in our lives, and all of us are created for human community in one form or another. Married couples are visible reminders that God's love is tangible, intimate, warm, and tender. All we have to do is reach out in love to others to discover our profound communion with our fellow human beings.

We can also bond with people we love who are unable to talk with us because of separation or various obstacles or blockages. For instance, suppose your relationship with your parents or siblings is still influencing you in a negative way. Maybe you cannot deal with the situation in real life: neither you nor they are capable of discussing the issues at hand because of old emotional wounds that prevent any progress. In the prayer of spiritual presence, however, you can open yourself to them, move beyond present obstacles, and experience healing. The love you experience from this powerful dialogue may indeed lead to the beginning of some brand-new relationships in your life.

Another way you can experience the spiritual presence of another does not involve words but consists of simply focusing on the other with attentive love. As you gently gaze at the other, you can become united with the other person in a deep spiritual union. Words are not needed. You can experience a profound spiritual presence capable of transforming your life. In April my eighty-five-year-old mother, Bridie, was hospitalized for more than two months with heart and kidney failure as well as serious respiratory problems and life-threatening infections. As I sat by her bedside, holding her hand each day, I felt closer to her than I had in my whole life. It was as if her spirit was dwelling within the depths of my soul. On this level I realized that nothing, not even death, could separate me from Mom. This enabled me to let go and place Mom in God's eternal embrace, where we are closer than we can imagine or dream.

For fifteen years, I worked in pastoral ministry in a small parish on a military post. Part of my job was to develop a pre-marriage program. In this process, I met several times with young engaged couples. I remember one young couple who became teary-eyed as they told me that they were facing a long separation because of military duty. They shared with me their survival plan to make it through this challenging time. They would each wear a locket with a picture inside, close to their hearts to remind them that they held each other close, no matter where they were.

One young mother once told me that her favorite time of day is in the evenings when she would rock her toddler to sleep. "As I hold my beloved child close and sing a lullaby to her, I experience the power of Love that is always within us, surrounding us and filling us with peace."

Several years ago George and Josephine, a delightful elderly couple, were part of my local small faith community. In spite of serious medical problems, George and Josephine brought a cheerful spirit to our Friday morning gatherings. "Where two or three are gathered in my name, I am there in their midst," Jesus tells us (Matthew 18:20 *Inclusive New Testament*). And so this little community discovered that one of the best ways to be with the God who will never abandon us is to share with one another in the midst of troubles.

One day Josephine had a stroke. For months, George spent almost every waking moment at her side, helping her in any way he could. After more months in a rehabilitation center, Josephine came home. George was ecstatic. Now they were together again at home where they belonged. Not long after this, George's cancer worsened. Now it was Josephine who remained by George's side, comforting and strengthening him. Every time I visited them, they shared that the only thing that mattered now was being together, offering their suffering to God and trusting in God's gracious will. A few months later George died, and within a year Josephine passed away. Like a diamond that sparkles more brightly with age, wear, and tender loving care, Josephine and George's love will never die. It is inspiring to me how courageous people, like George and Josephine, let go in the face of serious physical illness and, in their surrender, find peace in their journey to eternity's shore.

Recently, I completed a cable TV production on "The Healing Power of Prayer." For this program, I interviewed

George, a physicist who worked in the area of artificial intelligence. George told his story about being in remission from cancer for fourteen years. His cancer had just returned. During the taping he shared with us how he dialogued with God about his disease. He didn't know why this was happening to him, but he was radiant with joy because in this journey he encountered so much love in the midst of his illness. George told us that he experienced a vivid sense of God's presence surrounding him. It was like he had one foot in this world and one foot in heaven. He felt like a little excited child who had peeked in the candy store window and couldn't wait to get inside. His smile was contagious, and none of us will ever forget his last words to us: "All of life is gift, oh so many gifts!"

We are precious treasures created in the divine image who long for deep communion with our God. From the moment of our conception, God loves each one intimately, boundlessly, totally, passionately, as if he or she were the only person in the world. In fact, as God revealed to Teresa of Avila, "If I had never made the world, I would make it just for you!" Like swimming in the shimmering glow of moonlight, we can encounter divine grace lighting our path everywhere. This mystery of divine love surrounds us always. Our whole life is a wonderful journey into the amazing depths of an infinite love that will go on forever. Imagine! Every day God says, "I love you!" All we have to do is open up our spiritual awareness and we will hear this spoken in many natural ways. Like a fond mother, God is constantly saying, "My dear, dear child, I love you!"

Within this aura of love union we experience our communion with God and with everyone else. There are no clear boundaries. We can pray always. This is contemplative prayer: being present to the ever-presence of God, and to every other because all beings are enfolded in this energizing force. Contemplative prayer grounds our being in Love and enables us to see the face of God everywhere, even in pain and suffering. We become aware, as George did, that everything is gift.

I have developed a prayerful approach to experience deep love with God and with others.

PRAYER EXERCISES

Opening to Love

Go to a quiet place and relax your body. Begin with your head, face, and neck....Release any tension in these areas....Relax your shoulders, chest, arms, and hands....Release any tension in your back, stomach, hips, legs, and feet....

Be aware of your breathing. Inhale and exhale slowly for several minutes. One way to do this is to count to four as you inhale, hold your breath for the count of four, and count to four as you exhale.

Open yourself to the depths of God's love. Allow this boundless love to permeate your entire being.... Simply be in the presence of Love....No words are necessary....

Listen to God call you by name and tell you how much you are loved. Be still for a while and immerse yourself in the Divine Presence....

Be aware of any feelings, thoughts, sensations, and images that emerge as you reflect on God's love for you. Share these in a prayer dialogue with God.

Be aware of anyone in your life with whom you want to experience spiritual communion.

Share your feelings about this person with God.

Imagine God's holding this person close to the Divine Heart.

Imagine God's holding both of you in the Divine Embrace.

If you want, enter into a conversation with this person (these people). Be attentive to any feelings, thoughts, sensations, and images that emerge as you reflect on your relationship with her or him (them). Be aware of anything God wants to do to lead you to deeper intimacy. Record, if you wish, any insights from this encounter in your journal.

Encounter with a Friend or Family Member (Living or Deceased)

Choose someone with whom you are close and want to share deep love. Invite him or her to join you in this experience.

If you are present in the same place, lovingly look at your friend. If the person is not present, form a picture of her or him in your imagination.

Become aware of your spiritual connection with that person.

Share your feelings of gratitude and love for all this person means to you in a prayerful conversation with that person and/or with God.

Encounter with a Challenging Relationship
Choose someone you find difficult to love.

If the person is present, lovingly look at her or him. If the person is not present, form a picture of her or him in your imagination.

Begin a prayerful conversation with that person and/or with God. Share your feelings and thoughts with this person as openly and honestly as possible.

Spend some time, if appropriate, giving and receiving forgiveness.

Become aware of your spiritual bond with this person.

Open yourself to God's healing love in this relationship.

Encounter with a Loved One Who Has Died
Choose a member of your family, a friend, or another significant person who has died and for whom you still grieve.

Form a picture of your loved one in your imagination.

Begin a prayerful conversation with that person. Do not be afraid of expressing feelings of grief, anger, or loss with this person.

Forgive this person for leaving you.

Spend whatever time you need in giving and receiving forgiveness in this relationship.

Surrender this person into God's loving embrace.

Become aware of sharing a deep spiritual communion with the person.

Allow God's love to fill any emptiness or loneliness you still experience.

Encounter with a Special Mentor, Teacher, or Leader

Choose a person who has inspired you, encouraged you, affirmed your gifts, consoled you in your weakness.

If the person is present, lovingly look at her or him. If the person is not present, form a picture of her or him in your imagination.

Become aware of your spiritual oneness with that person.

Begin a prayerful conversation.

Share your feelings of gratitude with that person for all she or he did to encourage, help, or challenge you.

Now share with this person ways in which you are growing more like her or him in your relationship with others.

Encounters with Jesus, Mary the Mother of Jesus, or a Favorite Mystic or Saint

Whenever we pray to Jesus or with Mary or the mystics or saints, we believe that they are spiritually present to us and are willing to intercede or share their love, joy, hope, faith, passion, strength, and courage with us.

Imagine Jesus, Mary, and/or your favorite mystic or saint with you.

Become aware of your spiritual relationship with them. Become conscious that Jesus, Mary, or your favorite mystic or saint has been ministering to you, loving you, protecting you, helping you.

Begin a prayerful conversation.

Share your hopes, dreams, anxieties, joys, and failures with them.

Listen to their response to you. Be aware of any images, words, feelings, or insights that describe your experience.

Imagine yourself living in the fullness of God's love with all humanity and the entire cosmos in their presence.

If a word or phrase comes to mind, you may wish to repeat it as a mantra or prayer phrase.

As you do so, imagine yourself living as a person of passion and justice, like Jesus, Mary, or your favorite mystic or saint, in your relationships with others.

2

Live Joyfully and Peacefully Each Day

Bridget

My seven-year-old niece Katie and my four-year-old nephew Danny have shown me how to live peacefully and joyfully in the present moment. Through their eyes, I have come to appreciate on a deeper level the preciousness of life. Being with these delightful children makes me evermore conscious that God is in love with us and probably smiles a lot at our human antics—maybe even bursts out now and again in uproarious laughter.

I remember one sleepover at our house when Katie assigned the roles in our "pretend family": "I'm the mommy, and I'm having twins. Grandpa, you be the daddy; Danny, you are the dog; and Aunt Mary, you're my mommy." She then proceeded to put two small dolls under her shirt and asked, "Who's going to drive me to the hospital?" Of course, I volunteered. Moments later, Katie "gave birth" to babies Bridget and Patrick. It was amazing to watch her in action. First, she'd "give birth" by popping each one out from under her shirt, then she'd cuddle her "babies," nurse them, and put them to bed. As she did this, she was totally absorbed in loving her "children." As this game progressed, most of the dolls and bears around the house became Katie's "daughters" and "sons." On this particular evening, I think she had about a dozen "children"! You should have seen the room—we had "babies" everywhere. Meanwhile, Danny boy crawled around the floor, barking his little heart out. He took great pride in protecting his sister's "babies" from monsters. No wonder we did not get to bed until nearly midnight!

If we live like Katie and Danny—peacefully and joyfully in the present moment—we will encounter the face of God everywhere around us. We will recognize that God comes to us, not only in the happy times—in the new mother cuddling her babies, in the child riding her bike by herself for the first time—but also in the real struggles—in the cancer patient dealing with surgery and chemotherapy, in the unemployed neighbor who loses financial security, in a friend who wrestles with depression, in a teen's rebellion, in a parent's illness.

God is forever loving us and cries within us when we encounter enormous pain and suffering. Corrie ten Boom, a Nazi concentration camp survivor, reminds us that "there is no pit so deep that God's love is not deeper still." This means that no matter what trouble or suffering visits us, God is present, loving us fully in the experience of our deepest pain and losses. At times like these the soul expands and the spirit becomes strong. At times like these we can experience deep peace. After reading *Angela's Ashes* by Frank McCourt, my father, Jack, observed that this story brought back many memories of the poverty his family endured in the thirties in Ireland. "Yet," he smiled, "I know the human spirit can make it through anything—if love is present. My parents did the best they could. But I was determined that my children would have a better life, and this has given me peace and happiness."

"It has taken me so many years to be at peace in my own skin," Joan told me. Suffering from depression, Joan saw herself as disorganized and sloppy—a failure in everything she tried. Then one day she tried a healing-prayer exercise in which she dialogued with her undesirable parts. In her imagination, Joan sat in front of the fireplace in her living room and invited the Holy One to be with her and her undesirable parts. To her surprise, she "saw" God embrace her and hold her "weaknesses" close to the Divine Heart. "I felt wrapped in a blanket, and warmth spread all over my body," Joan shared. "I've never felt more loved in my life, and for the first time I experienced true inner peace and contentment." The next time I saw Joan several months had passed. I almost didn't recognize her. She had gone back to school and was embarking on a new career. She had a beautiful new dress and hairstyle. But her smile said it all—here is a radiant, confident, happy woman who knows she is beautiful.

Laughter heals the heart. If we can laugh—a real belly laugh—it means we don't take ourselves or our world too seriously. We know that—no matter how silly or ridiculous things are—all shall be well. Laughter reminds us that God loves us more than we can dream and cares for us always. We are never alone.

Our house is next door to a school. One of the high points of my day during the warm weather is to sit on our backyard swing with a cup of tea and listen to the children playing and laughing. Once in a while, when a ball comes flying over into our yard, I give myself permission to join in their fun by tossing the ball as high as I can back into the schoolyard.

My best teachers in the ways of love and laughter are my niece and nephew. They have shown me how to live joyfully on ordinary days. One school night I was invited to babysit Katie and Danny. My sister-in-law Nancy gave me my instructions. My brother simply smiled that knowing "brotherly" smile—the one that says "now it's your turn, Sis." I did come prepared. I had a plan. I would read them a story, say prayers, and tuck the little darlings into bed at their regular bedtimes. But when I shared my plan with the children, Katie pleaded, "Just one little game before we go to bed. Please, Aunt Mary, then we'll go to sleep real quick!" And so began a game called "Duck, Duck, Goose," Katie-style. This consisted of a high-speed chase across their bed. Guess who was the goose most of the time? There I was chasing two children, up one side of the bed and down the other, then around the bedroom for several minutes until I collapsed on the floor. If anyone could have observed us, they would have had a hard time figuring out who was having the most fun. I must confess, it felt great to be silly and enjoy the exhilaration of childhood. And I am in good company, since Jesus delighted in being with the children, and reproved his disciples for trying to keep them away from him. "'Let the children alone—let them come to me,' he chided. 'The kingdom of heaven belongs to such as these'" (Matthew 19:14 *Inclusive New Testament*).

For the past several years, my mother, Bridie, has been in and out of hospitals with life-threatening ailments. Several times the doctors had given up on her. Some days it was a struggle for her to eat, drink, take the amount of medicine prescribed, and do the therapy necessary to keep her mobile. Dad devised a way to get her to exercise. He would play their favorite Irish music and dance with her. She smiled, looking into Dad's eyes, and then slowly moved her feet a little to his rhythmic sway. This was amazing to us because before this Mom never liked to dance. But she did love to be held by her dear Jack. Is God preparing Mom and all of us for the cosmic dance we will be doing with God, the angels and saints, our relatives, and all creation throughout eternity? It is at moments like these that perhaps we can hear the divine love song that our hearts have always known and tap to the heavenly rhythm that our feet can't forget.

When we experience God's peace and joy in our lives, we often expand our images of God. This means that we not only know God's love in a new way, but we feel God's immeasurable tenderness in our hearts. We enter into an intimate relationship with Divine Love. This happened in my spiritual journey. As a young child, I saw God as a watchful judge who focused on my failures. I tried to please the God I loved by living up to the rules—the commandments and laws of the Church. As a teen, I encountered God as Lover. At this time, I focused on developing a close relationship with my Intimate Friend. In recent years, I have discovered God as Mother and as Holy Wisdom. Now I am exploring the feminine face of God and delighting in the healing and transforming presence of the Divine Feminine in my life. This is leading me to a deeper relationship with a loving God. I now feel more awe, more mystery, more intimacy, more peace and joy than I have ever experienced before in my holy encounters.

Living joyfully and peacefully is not always easy. I remember the panic I felt twenty-one years ago as if it were yesterday when the doctor told me that I had a growth on my vocal cords. The doctor recommended a month of voice rest. After the shock wore off, I struggled with my anxieties and wrestled with God. How would things turn out? Would I need surgery? Was this cancer? Would I need to give up my teaching career? I bargained with God and argued with God until I was weary of asking, "Why me? Why now?" In the process, I realized that there were no answers to my questions, but that God was with me, loving me into greater wholeness each day. As time passed by, I began what I call a "soaking prayer." Each day I would sit on the patio and image God's healing love flowing through my entire being. I imagined Jesus embracing me and healing not only my vocal cords but my fears of cancer and death. At the end of the month, not only had my vocal cords healed, but I had found a new sense of peace and trust that no matter what happened in my life, nothing would separate me from God's love.

No matter what challenges we face, we can find peace and joy everywhere and in every circumstance. The Bible reminds us hundreds of times *not to be afraid!* Yet how often do we find ourselves worrying about something? I, for one, am a worry expert. I have wasted lots of time being anxious about circumstances beyond my control. Sometimes I'll let go of the situation and give it to God; then, ten minutes later, I'll start fretting about the same thing again. It's at times like these that I imagine God is chuckling at me as I go back and forth with my worry. It will probably take me a lifetime to really get it! But I keep trying. It really is quite simple. All we have to do is open ourselves to receive the gift Jesus wants to give us in every situation in our lives: "Peace, I leave with you, my peace I give to you. I do not give to you as the world gives. Do not let your hearts be troubled, and do not let them be afraid" (John 14:27 *Inclusive New Testament*).

Living joyfully and peacefully involves us in a caring community. Sharing with friends, with family, with small faith communities provides us with a variety of ways to encourage, support, and love one another. A friend of mine, Maria, who was recently diagnosed with cancer, shared: "I could feel the support in the air before I went for surgery; it was tangible." Thomas Merton, a Cistercian monk and contemporary prophet, believed that spirituality is about being in communion with all creation. Merton used the image of the cosmic dance to describe a consciousness of God's presence in all aspects of life: "When we are alone on a starlit night, when by chance we see the migrating birds in autumn descending on a grove of junipers to rest and eat; when we see children in a moment when they are really children, when we know love in our own hearts…all these provide a glimpse of the cosmic dance."

Saint Paul found the key to happiness is being "rooted and grounded in love…able to grasp fully the breadth, length, height and depth of Christ's love and, with all God's holy ones, experience this love that surpasses all under-standing…" (Ephesians 3:17–19 *Inclusive New Testament*). Teresa of Avila prayed, "O Love that loves me more than I can love myself or understand." We, like Paul and Teresa, can celebrate the infinite, boundless love of God for us and live each day joyfully and peacefully in the Divine Embrace.

PRAYER EXPERIENCES TO LIVE JOYFULLY AND PEACEFULLY

There are various things each person can do to live more joyfully and peacefully.

- Be aware of the face of God in people you meet when you wait in line. Look around you and "see" the face of God in everyone. Pray for the needs of each person. Bless each person in your heart, and offer thanks for their presence in our world. Ask God to give them their hearts' delights.
- Compose a litany of intercession for those in need of peace, joy, and abundance in their lives. As you read the newspaper or watch the news, pray for the healing of violence, oppression, discrimination, and poverty.
- Volunteer to help those in need—for example, at a local shelter, a soup kitchen, a children's program, or a senior citizen group. In a prayer journal, reflect upon your experiences. Ask yourself, how did you encounter God's presence in the people you served? What is God saying to you through these encounters?
- Play with children and experience the exuberance of the child within you as you do so. Or choose your favorite fun activity and just enjoy it. As you do so, be aware that God is playing with you.
- Go to a funny movie or read a funny book and laugh uproariously. Let the laughter set your spirit free. Let it relax, free, and heal you. Reflect on God as a "Merry God," a "Joyful God" who is with you in happy and fun times.

- Enjoy a meal, a conversation, or an intimate moment with a loved one. Offer thanks to God and share with this person (these people) the things you are truly grateful for in your relationship(s).
- Repeat a form of the Jesus Prayer when you are performing ordinary tasks such as showering, working, eating, exercising, or trying to sleep: "Lord Jesus Christ, son of God, have mercy on me, a sinner"; or "Jesus, mercy"; or simply "Jesus" or "mercy." You can synchronize the Jesus Prayer with your breathing in and breathing out, that is, breathe in "Jesus," breathe out "mercy." Repeat the Jesus Prayer for people facing trouble or crisis.
- Recite the rosary, using all your senses to take in the sights, sounds, tastes, and smells of the world around you. One example: as you walk, pray the rosary for the marvels of creation that you see, touch, taste, hear, smell, and so forth.
- Imagine yourself playing with God....

  Delight fully in the experience....

  Sing, dance, laugh, rejoice in God's presence....

- Begin by spending a few minutes breathing deeply....

  Let go of all distractions and fears....

  If thoughts or feelings come, simply ignore them and let them float away as a twig floats down a quiet stream on a spring day....

Just relax and let yourself enjoy God's love surrounding you....

Be still and at peace....

Scripture Prayer Encounter

"Thus will you afterward find rest in her, and she will become your joy."

SIRACH 6:29
(New American Bible)

In the Hebrew, Greek, and Latin languages, "wisdom" is of feminine grammatical gender. Wisdom is the feminine aspect of the one God and is personified as a woman in Scripture. Biblical scholars suggest we use the word *Sophia*, a transliteration of the Greek word for wisdom, to connote a person and not an abstract mental concept.

Playful Prayer Encounter

Sophia's presence is holy ground. Wherever we are is holy ground. Reflect upon places where you recognize the presence of the feminine face of God.

How can recognizing Sophia's presence bring joy and peace in your life? in our world?

How can a sense of intimacy with the Divine Feminine help us become more whole?

Recall a time when you felt dynamic, creative, and full of confidence. What were you doing? Why was the experience so creative for you?

Take several deep breaths....Imagine that with each breath, your begin to release any tension you feel.... As you relax more deeply, your mind can become quiet and still....Invite your body to let go completely....Take time to be present to your surroundings....Be aware of what your senses experience....When you feel ready, go to a place where you can enjoy life....Take some time to have fun.... What are you doing? How are you feeling? Who is with you? Where are you?...

Be in awe of yourself....See yourself as a miracle... a reflection of Sophia's loving presence in the world....

Imagine yourself living the life you want to live as a caring, compassionate, vibrant person....Believe that nothing is impossible for you with Sophia's help....

Repeat one of the following prayer phrases, or mantras, to help you focus on Sophia's empowering presence in your life: "Sophia is my joy," "Sophia is my peace," "Sophia is my delight." You may make up your own....

Be aware of the ordinary events, the "daily miracles" of your life, such as a warm shower, hot coffee, smiles, friendly greetings from family members or coworkers....Reflect on how these and many other "little wonders" are holy ground for you....

Light a candle each day in a special place to remind yourself of the hope, peace, and joy that is all around you. Let the light from the candle help you to live the joy of Sophia more fully in the "holy ground" of life.

A Soaking Prayer in Jesus' Love

"Who will separate us from the love of Christ? Will [trouble], or distress, or persecution, or [hunger], or nakedness, or [danger], or [violence]? For I am convinced that neither death nor angels...nor things present, nor things to come... nor anything else in all creation, will be able to separate us from the love of God in Christ Jesus...."

ROMANS 8:35, 38, 39
(New Revised Standard Version Bible)

Before beginning, take a few moments to get comfortable and relaxed. Sit upright in a comfortable chair, feet flat on the floor. Or lay on a rug or mat.

Focus your attention on your breathing for a few minutes....Take a few deep, slow, abdominal breaths....Inhale....Exhale....Inhale....Exhale....
    Now, close your eyes....Relax your body gently by imagining a beautiful golden light starting at the top of your head and moving slowly down your

neck, spine, arms, legs, feet. Experience the warmth from this light filling your body with a feeling of well-being and vitality….

In your imagination, you see a stranger coming toward you….At first, you do not recognize this person….But now you know it is Jesus….He hugs you and holds you close….and sits beside you holding your hand….

Jesus invites you to share your feelings, thoughts, concerns, worries, troubles, or joys with him….Take as much time as you need….

Jesus has already experienced what you are going through and is with you now, loving you with compassion and strength….Experience the affection of Jesus for you….Soak in the healing, transforming love of Jesus for you….Let yourself be loved by Jesus….

Jesus gives you a special gift….Share this gift with all those you meet….

You are one with Jesus….You are one with all people and all creation….Become love to all those you meet, especially those who are suffering or in crisis…. Become, like Jesus, a radiant reflection of joy and peace….

Go in peace and be joyous, aware that nothing can separate you from the love of Jesus….

3

SHARE YOUR FEELINGS
WITH GOD

✍

Bridget

During a time of crisis in my life, my spiritual director offered me some wise advice: "Don't be afraid to tell God how angry you feel. God can handle all of your feelings, no matter how negative you may think they are." This began a slow but liberating journey for me. Anger has been a painful emotion for me to acknowledge. But in recent years I have learned to share my anger more openly about situations in which I felt I was treated unfairly by others. As I have done so, I have experienced a new sense of closeness with God and a better understanding of myself and other people. When I'm angry, sometimes I'll spend my prayer time complaining to God until I get it all out. Other times, I'll run with my anger. When I express my anger in these ways, I experience God's presence within helping me deal with the situation in a positive, life-giving manner. God is like an understanding friend who reminds me, "I love you as you are, no matter how angry or frustrated you feel. Trust me enough to share your outrage with me."

It is true. God accepts us the way we truly are. There is

no need to pretend that we are in control, or that life is fair, or that we have it all together. Our capacity to express our emotions honestly with God deepens our capacity for a passionate relationship with the Holy One. We can reveal to God a less than perfect face—the one with the blemishes and wrinkles that we sometimes cover up in order to hide from others. As we share all of ourselves with God—including our feelings—we will realize that God accepts us as we are and loves us more than we have ever imagined.

A few months ago a friend of mine had a heart attack. She told me later that when she awoke in the intensive care unit of the hospital, the first things she saw were tubes and wires attached all over her body. She felt pain in her chest and started to complain to God: "How could you let this happen to me? I thought you loved me and promised to take care of me. I don't want to die. Please, help me now!" After a while she drifted into a dreamlike state in which she thought she had died. In this place, she felt completely safe and peaceful. "When I awoke, I knew God was very close to me and had answered my prayer. I was no longer afraid to die."

Suffering and human misery are present everywhere we turn. Eighty percent of the world's population lives on 20 percent of its resources. Hunger, poverty, homelessness, and violence are a daily reality for many in the human family. In the United States we have consumed more of the earth's resources than most people would consume in several lifetimes. I don't know about you, but I feel guilty. My prayerful struggles with my own guilt have led me to meet with people who feel the same way. We support one another in our efforts to simplify our lives, pray for transformation of unjust structures, and take small, concrete steps to work for change in society. We do simple things like cook meals for shelters, help with hotlines, tutor children, visit the elderly, donate clothes and furniture to the needy in our neighborhoods, and lobby for a more just and inclusive society. It may not seem like a lot, but together we believe we can make a difference.

There are no answers to some of life's most painful questions. Why does a child die? Why do planes crash? Why does a young man in the prime of life get a malignant tumor? Why did the Holocaust and "ethnic cleansing" in Bosnia destroy millions of lives? Why do bad things happen to good people? When we experience loss and suffering, when we have no answers to human pain, sometimes all we can do is come to the cross and weep in the darkness—knowing we are not alone. God weeps with us.

One of the most tender experiences I ever heard about took place at a healing service. The team moved from person to person, laying hands on each one's head, asking what healing the person needed. When the team came to Elaine, she asked for healing of her guilt over a sexual sin that had happened many years ago during her adolescence. Later, Elaine shared her experience: "I closed my eyes and prayed with the team. The image of myself as a young girl after my first sexual encounter came to me. I was lying on my bed. Then I saw Jesus come through my bedroom door. He sat on my bed and looked into my eyes and gently caressed my face. I poured out my guilt and shame until I felt I had gotten it all out of me. He didn't say anything, but I never felt so much love and forgiveness in my life. A tremendous burden was lifted from my shoulders. I feel like a new person now."

I was sitting at my computer, focused on completing a chapter in a new manuscript. I heard Katie and Danny running down the steps, giggling and yelling, "Aunt Mary, play with us." So I stopped. I looked at them. I got up and turned on the music. The three of us did a fast jitterbug around the basement, grabbing dolls, bears, and chairs as extra partners. We were spinning, jumping, and laughing. When the music ended, I was gasping for breath but feeling great. Just then, their daddy arrived to pick them up. They gave me a quick hug and raced up the steps. I went back to my work. Suddenly it hit me: this is what life in the Spirit is all about—dancing our love with gusto. God invites each of us to participate in the dance of life, where we share our joys and sorrows with one another.

When I first met Steve, he was devastated after a bitter divorce from his wife, Monica. According to the custody settlement, he now could see his kids only once a month. In a letter he wrote, "When we were together, our home was filled with fighting, arguments, and turmoil. But I miss my children so much. Most days I feel so sad that I don't even want to get up. Work is my only distraction. I feel so lonely. Even God feels far away from me." In my return letter, I invited him to read the passages in Scripture in which Jesus faced loneliness. Several months went by and I heard from Steve again. He wrote, "The more time I spent sharing my pain with Jesus, the less time I felt sorry for myself. I am now able to look back and stop the blame game. I have been able to forgive Monica and myself. Now I really appreciate every minute I have with my children so much more."

One year ago I made a transition that has changed my life. I wasn't sure where the Spirit was leading, but I had an inkling that my future would involve a new spiritual adventure. At that time I asked God excitedly, "Can I spend the rest of my life savoring your passionate love and sharing it more fully with people everywhere?" I recorded my thoughts and feelings in a prayer journal. This helped me reflect on the Spirit's speaking within my heart. Here I discovered the strength, wisdom, and vitality I needed to pursue this new direction that suddenly unfolded in my life.

After a meeting nine months ago, my friend Rea suggested, "Bridget, why don't you start a spiritual TV talk show. You could call it 'Godtalk.'" At first, I thought this would be impossible. I felt like I was stepping off a cliff with no help in sight. But a voice within assured me, "Don't be afraid to jump; I'll catch you." So I took the plunge and landed in the arms of Love. I felt as if God had been talking to me through Rea. Doors began to open. I made a phone call to our local cable station and learned that the first step was to take the required classes. Since I was someone who could not even program a VCR, this was quite a challenge. Then a group of wonderful volunteers whom I had never met before came into my life to help with the program. Two of these young men, Jay and John, had previous television experience. So here I am now, a producer/host ready to roll with a series of five programs on "The Healing Power of Prayer" featuring interviews and prayer experiences on healing mind, body, and spirit, and a new series on courageous women in the Bible and Christian tradition. *Godtalk* is officially launched.

In the story of the two disciples' encounter with the Risen Christ on the road to Emmaus, "They said to one another, 'Weren't our hearts burning inside us as he talked to us on the road and explained the scriptures to us?'" (Luke 24:32 *New Revised Standard Version Bible*) The disciples' souls were stirred in the presence of Everlasting Love accompanying them on their journey. It took them a while, but they finally realized what had happened. God was with them in their sorrow, but they didn't recognize the Stranger walking beside them.

These disciples were slow on the pickup, just like we sometimes are. We don't always understand the events of our lives. We may be frightened or upset. We may be excited or happy. Can't you just see God smiling and laughing when we finally recognize the Stranger who comes to us in a number of disguises on our earthly pilgrimage. Then our hearts will burn within us too.

We can express our positive feelings of well-being, happiness, and joy as well as loneliness, sadness, and disappointment in our prayer. In the Bible we read about Miriam leading the Hebrew women in the dance of liberation in the Exodus story. Dancing for joy is a great way of celebrating life's large and small victories: "Then the prophet Miriam…took a tambourine in her hand, and all the women went out after her with tambourines and with dancing. And Miriam sang to them, 'Sing to God, for the Holy One has triumphed gloriously, horse and rider God has thrown into the sea'" (Exodus 15:20–21 *New Revised Standard Version Bible*). The Book of Psalms (all from the *New Revised Standard Version Bible*) is filled with prayers expressing every emotion under the sun. For example, Psalm 13 expresses the prayer of one in sorrow: "How long shall I harbor sorrow in my soul, grief in my heart day after day?" (2). Psalm 4 expresses joyful trust in God: "You put gladness into my heart, more than when grain and wine abound.

As soon as I lie down, I fall peacefully asleep for you alone….bring security to my dwelling" (7–8). Psalm 17 voices anger at injustice and asks for deliverance from persecution: "Hear a just cause, O God….hide me in the shadow of your wings from the wicked who despoil me….rise up, O God, confront them, overthrow them!" (1, 8–9, 13). Like the psalmist, we can compose our own passionate prayers, expressing our innermost feelings and desires to God.

The mystics and saints through the ages likewise prayed from their hearts, sharing their deepest emotions with God and with all creation. Francis of Assisi expressed his love for creation in joyful canticles to the earth's creatures, praising God for Brother Sun and Sister Moon. Brigid of Kildare was known for her happy spirit. In this grace she welcomed everyone to her table: "I should like a table of the choicest food for the family of heaven. Let the ale be made from the fruits of faith and the food be forgiving love. I should welcome the poor to my feast, for they are God's children. I should welcome the sick to my feast for they are God's joy. Let the poor sit with Jesus at the highest place, and the sick dance with the angels."* Catherine of Siena, Doctor of the Church, wrote with gratitude about the gift of her close friendship with Raymond of Capua. In a letter to Raymond she says that the foundation of love of neighbor is the love of God, and that love begets a faith that bonds us with another just as she and Raymond are bonded.

Like holy women and men through the ages we can open

---

*Robert Van de Weyer, "Brigid's Feast" from *Celtic Fire*. Found in Thomas Cahill, *How the Irish Saved Civilization* (New York: Doubleday, 1995) 174.

ourselves up and share our deepest feelings with God and with others. To sum up, we may want to keep in mind the following:

- First, God loves you with all your feelings. No feeling is unacceptable to God. Feelings are neither right nor wrong. They are morally neutral. God is big enough to handle all our feelings, even the negative ones like hate, anger, fear, envy, or guilt.
- Second, it is important to share our feelings with God as openly and honestly as we can. God, like our best friend, is a good listener and accepts us and our feelings as they are. Sometimes we may want to use our bodies and minds to express our feelings to God—like jumping for joy, or screaming out loud as we punch our anger out on a pillow. We can also talk out our anxieties by writing a worry list.
- Third, God will heal and transform the hurting areas in our lives if we simply ask and are open to being healed. God will exult over us as we express our joys, our happiness, our contentment in prayers of praise and thanksgiving.
- Fourth, sometimes we may need to seek professional help to handle deeply painful emotions. This can go hand in hand with the divine therapy that God does in healing the hurting places inside us.
- Fifth, celebrate—really celebrate—the love and happiness you experience on earth with all God's creatures. All your feelings are holy ground. Emotions, both negative and positive, can be powerful steppingstones leading you into the heart of God.

PRAYER WAYS TO SHARE
YOUR FEELINGS WITH GOD

A Guided Prayer Experience for Healing Shame
Use soft instrumental music in the background, and read or tape the prayer suggestions before you begin.

Breathe deeply for several minutes....

As you inhale, be aware of God's love embracing your entire being....

As you exhale, let go of all stress or tension....

Close you eyes and slowly and quietly repeat one of the following words or phrases for several min-utes: *God, Liberator, Healer, Shaddai, Faithful One, Spirit of Peace, Helper, Comforter.*

Remember a time in your life when you experienced shame or guilt. As you recall the situation, be con-scious of how you felt...what you did....Share your feelings openly and honestly with God....

God is the same yesterday, today, and forever. God can free you now from the guilt of the past and heal you completely now. Invite God to forgive and free you from your guilt and shame....

Imagine God embracing you and healing you....See yourself being filled with warmth and peace....

Observe God giving you the love and strength you
need to become whole—fully alive and in love with
God and others....Become a new creation....

Listen to God speak in the depths of your heart....
Let those words be emblazoned in your soul to remind you of God's tender mercies in your life....
Share your feelings, thoughts, and insights about
this experience with God....

In your imagination, do whatever feels comfortable
to celebrate God's healing love that you have experienced....

Whenever you feel ready, come back to the room,
a lot lighter than before you began this prayer.

A Psalm of Joy
*Pray this psalm or compose your own psalm expressing your
joy to God.*

Great is your compassion, O nurturing God.
You fill us with good things like hot rolls and
    coffee each day.
You kiss away the wounds of our hearts.
In our tears and fears we experience
    your tender love.
    Response: Sing to God for joy.

Wondrous are your marvelous deeds in our lives.
You hold us close to you in tribulation and trial.

You free us from oppression
that we may walk always in the light
  of your freedom.
  Response: Sing to God for joy.

Tender is your touch and warm is your smile.
You draw us with your transforming grace.
You connect us with one another
that we may praise you forever as one people united
in love and committed to service.
  Response: Sing to God for joy.

Glorious and gracious is your presence in our world.
You help us care for Earth's creatures,
  the fruit of your womb.
You fill us with your wisdom and strength
that we may rejoice with all creation forever
  in your presence.
  Response: Sing to God for joy.

Praying Your Feelings through Art

Paint, draw, sketch, or use clay to express your feelings.

Look at your drawing, painting, or sketch....

Spend several minutes breathing in and out your feelings. One way of doing this is the following:

With each breath, take in your feelings....

Breathe in your joy, peace, freedom, anxiety,
fear, hate....

As you do so, give your feelings as they are
to God....

Praying Your Feelings through Scripture

"My compassion grows warm and tender."
HOSEA 11:8
(New Revised Standard Version Bible)

"Peace I leave with you, my peace I give to you. I do not
give to you as the world gives. Do not let your hearts be
troubled and do not let them be afraid."
JOHN 14:27
(New Revised Standard Version Bible)

The symbols, stories, and images of the Bible give us
many possibilities for sharing our feelings with God.

Recall that God wants you to experience boundless love,
joy, and peace in the Divine Heart. God loves you infinitely, passionately, totally. Each of us is held close to all
those we love in the Divine Heart. Indeed, all the human
family is profoundly united in love in God's heart. This
wondrous mystery can fill us with awe, wonder, and love.
We have nothing to fear.

Quiet yourself. Relax. Breathe in deeply the boundless love of God for you....Breathe out deeply God's
love for all people and for all creation....Breathe
in Divine Peace.....Let go of anxiety and fear....

Read the Scriptures….Listen as God reveals the desires of the Divine Heart for you and for every creature….

Share the desires and feelings of your heart with God….

Compose a litany of thanksgiving or a spontaneous prayer expressing your feelings of gratitude for the gift of God's love and peace in your life….Or offer the following prayer:

> Divine Lover, I rejoice in your passionate love present in me and all around me— everywhere—and in everyone. Hold me close forever to your heart. Here I will discover deep joy and true serenity. Amen.

Pray for all people throughout the world who are in turmoil. As each group comes to mind, imagine them in a large, cosmic heart surrounded by love and peace….See them being transformed by God's love….Now imagine all people and all creation living together in peace, justice, and harmony….What kind of world would this be? Decide on something you can do to make the world a more peaceful place….Perhaps you can begin by performing an act of kindness for a person or creature near you now….

4

BLESS THE MESSES

Regina

The story is told of the Master Artist who moved from one of his protégés to the next, scanning their progress, giving a suggestion here, a touch of the brush there. Suddenly, he stopped at the canvas of a pupil who had turned away from the work in huddled misery! Across the canvas a large scar of scarlet paint spelled the final ruin of a nondescript pastoral scene.

A gentle hand rested on the shoulder of the despairing student. A quiet, sensitive voice murmured, "All is not lost!—Watch!" With a few deft strokes the oil was transformed. The scarlet scar had become a russet sunset. The mediocre was transfigured: a floral woodland spring burst upon the canvas through the strokes of the Master Artist.

That is what God does all the time with our blunders! Our God blesses the messes! This is the wonder of the resurrection principle in our daily, humdrum lives. Our Christian faith experience gives us the secure hope that God can and will bring forth the best from each of our sincere efforts. But more than this—even our blunders God not only forgives, but transforms.

Of course, there are relatively little messes in life, and there are gigantic, seemingly hopeless messes. I think of all the times I *almost* forgot something that could have been crucial to our parish program—like forwarding the funding request for an upcoming event. Invariably, someone filled up the memory gap, just in the nick of time! I've gotten used to recognizing this "touch of the Master Artist" with a sigh of gratitude.

However, it's the seemingly impossible solutions of the gigantic, involved, convoluted messes that shock me into profound awe. Mom and Dad's separation and divorce and Dad's second marriage were just such a gigantic mess! It caused the disruption of a twenty-year relationship, the disintegration of our family, and a lifelong scarring of the lives of their two children. Now, fifty years later, I still see in my slowly integrating being some remnant scars of this family bombshell. What can be a bigger mess than a family's destruction, and the confused emotions and outraged hatreds it leaves in its wake?

I still affirm that we have a God whose goodness and love-power is so immense that God can and does bless even the most hopeless mess when we turn it over to God. Our family blessing began when Dad was told he had cancer of the spine, a terminal condition. God transformed the negative situation of Dad's final illness into a significant spiritual experience that changed my father's whole outlook on life and death and simultaneously brought reconciliation and resolution to our broken, hurting family.

"God talked to me all night, Regina; what does this mean?" Dad was clearly agitated. Since he was a thorough agnostic, looking on the Creator as merely a disinterested force, I was inclined to discount what he was saying; but he was adamant. *"God talked to me all night, I tell you!"*

"What did God say?" I asked.

"It wasn't words; but it was God, all right. God showed me all the relationships of my life as in a great map, and how misunderstanding and human weaknesses had interfered and broken these ties. What does this mean?"

"Well, Dad," I answered, "you have always ridiculed people who talked about a spiritual experience; but now you have had one, and you know that it is real, and that God does love and care and is very, very close to you."

In the weeks that followed Dad kept delving into the mystery of his experience. He talked to his nurses about it. He talked to hospital chaplains of all denominations. He started going to the chapel for services. And he asked to see my mother!

"Mom," I said to her gently that night, "Dad has terminal cancer of the spine, and he would like to see you. Do you want to go?"

"Yes!" Her response was swift and certain. "What do you think I should wear? Would this dress look best, or should I wear one of my pantsuits? And I need to get my hair done!"

This, too, was a transformation. Since her divorce twenty-five years before, and during the separation that preceded it, Mom couldn't be in the same room with my father. One didn't try to force the issue because her nerves literally tore her apart. Her hands would shake; her body would shake, and she would sob. Yet here she was, peacefully, even excitedly, anticipating their meeting!

"Sally," I told my stepmother, "I'm bringing my mother to the hospital to see my father."

The moment of encounter was almost too much for me. For twenty-five years I had prayed that my father would come to know our God as a *personal God,* transcendent beyond all human foibles, yes, but intimately, wondrously immanent, involved in the warp and woof of our individual lives in an immense, unconditional love-embrace. I had also prayed for our family, for some kind of miraculous healing. Now, here it was! The prayed-for answered in that precious *Present Moment.* And how graciously God had let me be a participant in that moment!

I didn't listen to what was said. Mom and Dad talked at his bedside. I waited in the hall. Mom told me afterward that he recounted his God-experience and said that if he had only known thirty years ago what he knew at that moment they would still be together; there would never have been a divorce.

Mother was at peace! Daddy was at peace! My soul "exalted in God our Savior!"

The climax came at Dad's funeral. Mother leaned over and kissed my stepmother, Sally!

God blesses the messes, great and small. When God blesses, everything is transformed! The canvas of life loses its blemishes, and the Great Artist converts our faulty brush strokes with a single touch.

PRAYER WAYS TO YIELD YOUR "MESSES" TO GOD FOR BLESSING

Affirm to the ever-present God who dwells in the depth of your own heart, "I know you, God, that you are All Goodness, that you care for me, and that you can and do bless and transform the messes we make in our lives. Take this mess of mine (*name it*) into your hands." Affirm God's goodness and ability to transform over and over—*gently!*

God is *always already there* in our lives (Karl Rahner), at work before we are even aware of it. Therefore, ask God to show you which "mess" in your life God is *already* in the process of mending. Yield this mess into God's care. Do not try to protect it or control it any longer. *Let go* of it into the Master Artist's hands.

Reflect on little times in your life when things could have really botched up but when, *just in time*, you remembered or someone intervened. Thank and praise God now for being the blesser of these little messes.

Reflect on a time or times when a really gigantic mess was affecting your life but when God's intervention turned things around. How many of these are part of your life history? How often did you recognize God's touch and give thanks? You can do so now, even if you failed to recognize your "rescue" in the past. Enter into a time of thanksgiving to God for each divine intervention you have experienced in your life. You might make a little litany of these as they occur to you. For example:

> For your wonderful care of me at the moment of
> birth—Loving God, thank you.
> For pulling me through (some severe childhood
> illness)—Loving God, thank you.

For giving me a really good friend in ———, with
  whom I could share some of my deepest feelings, when I was really hurting for friendship—
  Loving God, thank you.
For moments when you let me know you are here,
  loving me—Loving God, thank you.
For leading me to follow the inspiration to ———
  (do or be or become)—Loving God, thank you.

Be creative in composing your own litany!

If there is a really big mess affecting your family or your
life at this moment, turn to your ever-present, loving God,
hold it in your hands, and hand it over into God's hands.
See yourself making this transfer. Tell God, "It's yours now,
God. I can't do anything about it. It's too hopeless from
where I stand; but for you nothing is hopeless!" Then thank
God for blessing this mess.

Invite God to be totally in charge of your life and actions. Yield to God's healing action for a few moments as
you delight to be resting in the arms of your infinitely caring God!

God's Word Gives Us Assurance of God's Desire to Transform Our Messes

"Your God is in your midst…[and] will rejoice over you with
gladness, [and] will renew you in love….I will remove
disaster from you, so that you will not bear reproach for it."

ZEPHANIAH 3:17–18
(New Revised Standard Version Bible)

Reflect on this promise. Realize that it is meant for you, personally. There are actually three promises in the passage: (1) God is in your midst—right here, now, for and with you. (2) God will *renew* you in love. If you have strayed and have not always been faithful, if you feel *unworthy*, don't fret. God *promises* to renew you! Talk to God about this promise and how much you need it. (3) God "will remove disaster from you so that you will not bear reproach for it!" What a relief! Tell God about the mess and how afraid you are of the outcome. Ask God to take over the situation *and* your heart!

"I will stand at my watch post and...I will keep watch to see what God will say to me....Then God answered me and said: 'Write the vision: make it plain....For there is still a vision for the appointed time....If it seems to tarry, wait for it; it will surely come; it will not delay.'"

HABAKKUK 2:1–3
(New Revised Standard Version Bible)

Reflect on the promise in this Scripture, which also demands of us patience in our *watching* and *waiting*. Practice perseverance in your prayer for God to take control of the situation you cannot resolve yourself. The Scripture says, "God answered me." Expect that God *will* answer your need. You do not know when, but you can be sure that it will be at the right moment. And when that moment arrives, you will be filled with the joy that comes from experiencing God active in your life. Think about these things as you reread the scriptural passage.

"The truth of the matter is, if you ask Abba God for anything in my name, it will be given to you....Ask, and you
will receive so that your joy may be complete."

JOHN 16:23–24
(*INCLUSIVE NEW TESTAMENT*)

These words are taken from the passage that the writer
of John's Gospel includes in Jesus' Last Supper homily to
the disciples. The promise speaks to the heart when we
ache for an answer to our deepest need in times of distress.
Don't be afraid, then, to take Jesus at God's word, and to
entrust *your* need to Abba God *in Jesus' name*.

What does "in Jesus' name" mean? In the understanding of gospel times a person's name was extremely significant as incorporating *the person himself/herself;* the *name*
included that particular person's significant call and direction in life. We might reflect that *Jesus* means "Yahweh is
in the process of saving/healing." God *is* healing us, even
as we ask. God *is* taking control of the situation, even as
we turn it over to God in our helplessness. In this spirit,
talk to God about your need.

5

CELEBRATE YOUR
SPIRITUAL EMPOWERMENT

Bridget

It was one of those beautiful days. The sun was shining brightly. The clouds looked like fluffy white pillows resting on the soft blue bed of the sky. The breeze was warm and gentle. I was opening the window and enjoying the view when the phone rang. It was my friend Sarah on the other end of the line. She told me about a recent family gathering at which her sisters and brothers had spent hours arguing over silly little things that had happened years ago. "By the time it was over," Sarah complained, "I was so annoyed that I just wanted to get out of there. You'd think we'd get along a lot better now that we are adults."

It is not unusual to feel irritated with members of our family. Sometimes it helps to remind ourselves that there are no perfect families like those of *Ozzie and Harriet* or *Leave It to Beaver* fame. All of us are wounded and on a journey to wholeness. Yet love is inside us and all around us, and we can choose to be an instrument of peace. When we live in God's love, we have unlimited potential to forgive, heal, encourage, and love others.

When we are held prisoner by anger, resentment, or blaming others, we can't see the forest for the trees. Everything revolves around *our* needs, hurts, and pain. The prayer attributed to the thirteenth-century mystic Saint Francis of Assisi suggests an attitude shift that can set us free: "God, make me an instrument of your peace. Where there is hatred, let me sow love; where there is injury, pardon;...where there is sadness, joy." In other words, if we want joy, peace, and happiness, we need to live compassionately.

We cannot change others, any more than they can change us. All we can do is love others where they are and support their growth. As Sarah attempted to work on her own spiritual development, she realized that she was becoming a new person. "When I discovered what a struggle it was to change myself, I became more understanding toward my family. I realized that a lot of things that bothered me about them—anger, greed, jealousy—were in me."

This process of unleashing our potential involves a new way of thinking and a deeper way of loving. Young couples think that they have experienced the fullness of love on their wedding day and honeymoon, while in reality they have just planted the seeds that, if carefully tended, will blossom into a magnificent love in the years ahead. Becoming the beloved of another is a lifetime commitment. As we juggle the responsibilities of families and jobs, pursue careers, and nurture relationships, we can become more patient and gentle with ourselves and those around us. After all, we are all "works in progress" who are becoming the beloved of others.

Like Mary, the Mother of Jesus and the disciples of Jesus who received the fullness of the Spirit on Pentecost, we too can proclaim the fiery sparks of passionate gospel living every day. When we open ourselves to the Holy Spirit's presence in our lives, miracles can happen. Pentecost is a reality that we can experience every day. The promise of Jesus is the source of our spiritual empowerment: "You will receive power when the Holy Spirit has come upon you, and you will be my witnesses…to the ends of the Earth" (Acts 1:8 *Inclusive New Testament*).

One eve of Pentecost about ten years ago, Regina and I were traveling on the Southeast Freeway in Washington, D.C., when we heard a loud thud and our car came to a sudden stop. While traffic was speeding by us, we could see a police cruiser pull up right behind us. The officer approached us and asked us what was the matter. "Our wheel fell off," Regina replied. The officer shook his head in disbelief that we had not had a serious accident. Another car stopped behind the cruiser, and a man walked up to us and handed us our tire, which he had chased down the freeway. After thanking both men for helping us, Regina and I praised God for protecting us. The officer smiled and said: "This is amazing grace at work for sure." Then he called ahead for a tow truck and stopped traffic on the busy thruway so that our car could be turned around and towed away. Regina and I have told this story to many people over the years. We believe that God's saving power is always with us. We especially need it when we get in a car!

We have often joked about our poor sense of direction—which means that on most trips we get lost at least once. Traveling together, we are a "dynamic duo" open to adventure. Our infamous detours remind us that we are not alone. God is very close to us whether we are on the right or wrong road. Through our meanderings, we have learned to enjoy the present moment of travel as a time of divine encounter. Just as life sometimes takes us in directions that we did not anticipate, we can be at peace if we realize it is all part of God's plan. Regina and I have discovered that when we let go and let God lead us, even our wrong turns become occasions of blessings that can energize us. It causes us to spend more time together seeking and searching for the right road, and as we do this, God often speaks to us through each other's ideas and insights. Sometimes we dream new dreams and share new visions for religious life or for women's ministry in the Church.

Alice's story reminds me that God uses others to ignite the fire of hope in our hearts. One day Alice told me that her husband had criticized her and contradicted her opinions for years. She made excuses for his behavior: "He only hit me once. It was my fault. I didn't listen to him. I was too preoccupied with the children." After months of therapy, Alice realized that her lack of self-love was a problem. What changed her life was when she realized that she was worthy of love: "I asked God to help me see my potential. Some members of my support group told me that they saw me as intelligent, caring, and a good listener." Their message motivated Alice to go back to school and eventually to become a counselor. Now she leads women's empowerment seminars and works in the area of career transitions and life changes. Hundreds of people have been inspired by Alice's story, and their lives have been enriched by her programs.

Women in our society need to affirm their self-worth and celebrate their empowerment. The media consistently devalue women by sending negative messages about women's bodies and sexuality. When everything we see and hear tells us that women need to look or dress a certain way to attract men, or have certain makeup or clothes to be beautiful, we are being sold a bill of goods that leads to emptiness. Women come in all shapes and sizes. God accepts us as we are and calls us "beloved." We need to discover our true identity in the depths of our souls. We are beautiful and gifted because we are created in the image of God. The words of Hildegard of Bingen, the medieval mystic, reflect our nobility and brilliance: "In this circle of earthly existence, you shine with radiant light so finely it surpasses understanding. God hugs you. You are encircled by the arms of the Mystery of God."

Each of us can be messengers of the in-breaking of God's reign. We can discover ways to unleash the Spirit of God's love right where we are. Sometimes it involves visiting a friend who has lost a loved one, or cooking a meal for a sick neighbor, or fixing a leaky faucet for an elderly parent, or smiling at the next person we meet. Sometimes it involves taking risks such as sharing your vulnerability with others. For me, it has meant sharing my soul journey through books. Ten years ago, if anyone had told me I would have published sixteen books by now, I would have laughed in disbelief and said, "That's impossible!" Yet as I opened myself to the Holy Spirit's guidance, it became clear that God was calling me to share with people I'd probably never meet this side of heaven my personal relationship with the loving God who is transforming my life.

We can celebrate our spiritual empowerment by being a radiant reflection of God to our sisters and brothers in the world. Like Jesus, each of us has been chosen: "The Spirit of God is upon me because the Most High has anointed me to bring good news to those who are poor. God sent me to proclaim liberty to those held captive and recovery of sight to those who are blind, and release to those in prison—to proclaim the year of Our God's favor" (Luke 4:18–19 *Inclusive New Testament*). By our baptisms we have been empowered by the Spirit for ministry to others. Jesus reminds us that there is no love for God without love for neighbor. "This is my commandment, love one another as I have loved you" (John 15:12 *Inclusive New Testament*).

Through human relationships we are meant to experience intimacy with God and spiritual empowerment. The more we love one another, the more we are energized to love God. Other people are meant to be icons of God's presence shining brightly, like warm sunshine in our lives. Like a flower that blossoms when watered by the spring rain, so our deepest selves grow when someone loves us. Warm human love helps us experience what God's intimate love feels like. If I've never known human tenderness, how can I appreciate God's infinite love?

Yet human love has its limitations. I can never completely know or be known by another person. Each of us is a mystery—even to ourselves. Only God can love us perfectly. Only God can make up for the love that we needed in our relationships but did not receive. Only God can liberate us from the walls that separate us from others; only God can heal the hurts that fester in the depths of our souls. God's love alone can free, heal, and empower us to love with the freedom of the children of God. Saint Augustine had it right when he recognized the hole in the human heart that could only be filled by the Holy One. It is true indeed, as he said, that our hearts are restless until they rest in God. It is here that we can find our lasting home. God alone can fill the thirsts of the human heart for peace, love, and fulfillment. Jesus invites us to come and drink from the Fountain of Life: "Any who are thirsty, let them come to me and drink! Those who believe in me, as the Scripture says, 'From their innermost being will flow rivers of living water'" (John 7:37–38 *Inclusive New Testament*). What more could we ask for?

This chapter provides three approaches to celebrate your spiritual empowerment. The first one consists of utilizing your intuitive processes to help you tune in to your higher purpose and discover your creative power. In this model you create prayers that reflect the Spirit speaking in the depths of your being. The second approach leads you in a contemplative experience of yourself as a new creation. The third approach provides a psalm to celebrate God's Spirit in your life. Prayer approaches like those can help you to celebrate your spiritual empowerment. Each one invites you to open a window through which you can glimpse grace everywhere, every day of your life.

PRAYER EXPERIENCE TO CELEBRATE SPIRITUAL EMPOWERMENT

Choose an area in your life in which you desire to lift your spirit higher. Where are you being challenged? Where do you want to take risks? Listen to your inner wisdom and find your creative spirit.

Imagine yourself living as if you have exceeded your expectations....

Discover Your Creative Power

Write a prayer stating your desire to discover your creative power, your inner source of vitality, passion, energy, life.

Some of the ones I use are "I rise with Beauty, radiant with Love"; "I can do all things in God who strengthens me"; "Desire of my Soul, empower me"; "Wisdom of God, guide me to challenge injustice."

Repeat your prayer often. This repetition deepens the thought patterns and releases behaviors that raise your awareness of the Spirit speaking in the depths of your being. When I repeat the words "I rise with Beauty, radiant with Love," for example, before I begin a speech to a large audience or in front of the television cameras, I become centered, calm, and confident, and I experience God's love energizing me.

Record any thoughts, feelings, insights, images, and intuitions that flow from this prayer experience in painting, poetry, song, dance, clay, or any favorite artistic expression. One time I turned on praise music and painted the bright colors and feelings of joy and exuberance as I reflected on my creative power. Another time I danced with my creative spirit. As I swirled and swayed to the music, I experienced the Holy Spirit releasing my inhibitions and leaping within me. Later, as I reflected on this dance, I knew the Spirit was freeing me to connect more with God's Divine Energy within me and around me in the beautiful earth.

Share your creative power with family, friends, neighbors, strangers. I often "try on" my new spiritual insights with people who are close to me before I present them to a larger audience at retreats and conferences around the world. This helps me to receive feedback and affirmation. I have discovered that sometimes those closest to us are wise guides in assisting us in the process of spiritually discerning the new gifts the Spirit brings into our lives. All we have to be is open to the voice of God speaking in those around us.

Experience Yourself As a New Creation

Lie or sit down comfortably, close your eyes, and breathe deeply....Breathe in and out slowly and deeply from the abdomen....As you breathe in and out, be aware of your body....Begin at the top of your head...your face...ears...nose...eyes... mouth...chin....Move downward, focusing on each body part to the very soles of your feet....Inhale deep breaths and send oxygen to every cell in your body....As you exhale, imagine blowing out any stress, tightness, or pain you find in your body....

As you breathe in and out, imagine the Spirit filling you with love, peace, kindness, self control, gentleness, wisdom, generosity, or whatever your heart desires....

Be aware of any areas in which you need to experience forgiveness, healing, freedom, love....

Invite the Spirit to speak to your heart....Is God calling you to be a new creation, to do great things?...to witness the gospel in a powerful way?...to let go of old resentments and hostilities?...to become the beloved of others?...to live the life of the Spirit in its fullness?...to take some risks for the gospel? Imagine yourself doing great things for God....Picture yourself loving passionately, acting justly, walking humbly with your God....

Open yourself to the infinite, tender love of God for you....Listen to God praise you for your gifts.... Listen as God calls you by name and expresses gratitude for your gifts ("*your name*, I bless you for reflecting my kindness in your smile...my generosity in your service to the elderly/young/homeless...")....

Look into a mirror—either a real or imaginary one—and see yourself as God's beloved, truly possessing everything you need to be peaceful and happy....As you open yourself to this experience, be aware of any insights, images, feelings, or thoughts that emerge....

Give thanks that you are the handiwork of God... your body is God's special dwelling place...your mind and spirit reflect the thoughts, feelings, and insights of God's Spirit....Write a poem, psalm, or prayer of thanksgiving....

Take all the time you need to move your awareness back to the place where you are....When you are ready, open your eyes, stretch your body gently, and smile as God's new creation....

Become a Thankful Person

Pray this sample poem that might help you express your thanks to God:

I Am Yours, My God

O Love that flows within me always,
I am your special creation, new each day
in the refreshing springs of your love:
You speak to my womanspirit each day
love words that whole my soul and heal my heart.
"I love you."
"You are mine."
"You are my delight."
"I am loving through you."
Living Water, I praise you for the fountain of your
love welling up within me, lifting me higher….
I am yours, my God, forever and ever.

A Psalm to Celebrate God's Spirit in Your Life

Pray this psalm or create your own to give voice to your celebration of the Holy Spirit's activity in your life.

God, your love dazzles me. Your divine energy
    revitalizes my spirit.
New possibilities, fresh hopes, daring dreams
    are emerging.
Your Spirit cherishes my creative power.
Sometimes I worry, become anxious,
    and lose my way.
Cling to me in my times of struggle.
Your love melodies sing and dance within me,
    all around me
now and forever.
Blessed are you, God of my heart.

You understand me fully and love me totally
even when I don't know where I am going
    or how I am getting there.
You show me the path to wisdom and fullness
    of joy in your presence.
Gentle Spirit,
your forgiveness delivers me from evil and
    heals the wounds of sin in my soul,
free me from all misplaced priorities that I may
    center my life on the fullness of your love.
God, you are my strength and peace,
    the joy of my life.
You have poured out your Spirit on me.
May I see visions and dream dreams
    as your prophets and saints of old.
Today I will expect a miracle.
I will soar on eagles' wings
as you lead me, O Promised Hope,
to show your compassion
to everyone and everything—aware that in you,
    we are all one.
Your life-giving Spirit appears in every face and
    in every place.
May my heart be wide open to loving and
    being loved.
Bless my hands this day that they may reach out
    to touch tenderly the hurt in others' lives.
Bless my feet this day that they may travel the
    path to serve another with kindness and
    generosity.
May your amazing grace overflow
    in all my encounters.

6

FORGIVE AND ASK
FORGIVENESS—TAKING FLIGHT

Regina

For how many centuries have people hungrily looked into the depths of the sky and longed, like the eagle, to take flight? How many people attempted to create a "flying machine" that would enable them to break free from our earth-bound state and float among the clouds? Greek mythology records this universal longing of humankind but comments on it as a sin of wanting to be "God"; hence the protagonist who creates wings is doomed to failure from the start, and we are not surprised when the story tells that the waxen wings melt in the heat of the sun.

Christians enjoy a much safer way to break loose from our bonds and fly free! Jesus gives us the formula when he states, "If you bring your gift to the altar and there remember that your sister or brother has a grudge against you, go to be reconciled to them, and *then* come and offer your gift" (Matthew 5:23–24 *Inclusive New Testament*); and again, "Love your enemies, and do good to them…you'll be rightly called children of the Most High, since God is good even to the ungrateful and the wicked" (Luke 6:35 *Inclusive New Testament*).

Jesus gives us two interrelated prescriptions for freedom: forgive others freely and ask forgiveness speedily.

I do not find either of these easy!

As a child, I simply could not come right out and say, "I'm sorry!" Somehow it felt too self-demeaning. I simply could not get myself to verbalize the words *I'm sorry, please forgive me!* I recall visiting my father as a fifteen-year-old. (Mom and Dad were divorced, and I got to visit Dad in the summer when school was out.) I was taking organ lessons at the time and playing for the children's choir, so Dad arranged with the local pastor for me to practice on the church organ during my visit. I was in the midst of practice one day when another teenager accosted me in the choir loft and, in very unfriendly terms, questioned my right to be there. The next day, however, she approached me and said, "I'm really sorry I talked to you that way yesterday. I think I was jealous of you, but I'm sorry. Please forgive me!" I was taken aback! Not so much by the encounter as by the fact that she had learned to do, with relative ease, what I could never do—speak the words *I'm sorry!* I would *be* sorry and *feel* sorry, but I could not *say*, "Please forgive me!" Instead, I would *do* something for the person, hoping they would get the inference that the *doing* meant I was sorry. This teenage girl taught me a lot about what was missing in my maturing process—the ability to take responsibility for a negative action, to feel sorrow, and to express that openly!

Of course, I forgave her. I couldn't have done otherwise, her request was so humble. I found out what time she wanted to practice the organ and made my practice schedule accommodate hers. The whole situation became a winwin relationship because she had had the humility and maturity to express her regret that she had behaved badly.

It was many years later that the lesson this teenager taught me bore fruit in my own life to the point that I began to *ask* forgiveness and not just *act out* that desire. Eventually I did reach sufficient maturity to say the magic words *I'm sorry.*

Then came another memorable bout with the humility of asking forgiveness. I attended a Charismatic Conference at Notre Dame, Indiana, around 1977. A Spanish-speaking delegation was present in the amphitheater for the closing Mass. They had arrived late, and there had been some confusion and unpleasantness about seating them and caring for their needs. When their presence was announced from the podium, negative electricity spiked the air—you could *feel* the hostility. That is, until the priest who was emcee stepped to the microphone. "There has been a lot of negligence and lack of caring for the needs of our brothers and sisters from Central America," the speaker said. "We acknowledge this un-Christlike behavior and are sorry it happened." Still the negative vibes radiated. "In the name of all here present, brothers and sisters, I ask your forgiveness. Please forgive us for failing to make you feel welcome! Forgive us!" There was a moment of breathless silence, and then, from their part of the stadium came the sound of clapping, softly at first, then thunderously! They had forgiven. The time of prayer could go on now, with bridges rebuilt, as if the negligence had never happened.

This time I said to myself, "It's not just enough to say, 'I'm sorry!' We need to *request*, 'Please forgive me!'" This new insight challenged me because by this time I could say, "I'm sorry." I just couldn't go the one step further to say, "Please forgive me!"

My third memorable lesson about forgiveness enabled

me to see the mysterious power of apology to bear fruit across the years. This time I was at the graveside of my wonderful Aunt Fran. During her later years we had taken ever so many trips together. One of these had been to Harper's Ferry, West Virginia, the site of the firing of the first shot during the Civil War for the freeing of the slaves— the historic spot of John Brown's raid. Here, at Aunt Fran's graveside, my friend, Sister Mary Emma—the only black sister in my community—recalled her strongest memory of Aunt Fran.

"When we went to Harper's Ferry together," she said, "Aunt Fran, Regina, and I, Regina asked me how my parents had come to live in Norristown, Pennsylvania. I told her my grandfather had run away from southern Maryland at the age of ten, to escape slavery.

"Regina asked if I had ever really known my grandfather." [Yes, I had asked this, hoping against hope that this was just a hand-me-down story. Otherwise, here was one of my contemporaries whose *grandfather* had lived during the Civil War! That would bring slavery too close to my own era for comfort!]

"I told her that I had been Granddad's favorite grandchild; and that he had asked, in his final illness, if I might come home from the convent to see him before he died. My community arranged for me to travel to see him that last time.

"Then, it was that Aunt Fran said the thing I will never forget! 'Emma,' she murmured in her soft, Virginia drawl, 'My grandfather was a slave owner. He was always good to his slaves, but he did have them to run the plantation. We know now how wrong that was! No human being should ever think he can *own* another person. We know that now;

but they didn't realize, in my grandfather's day, how evil slavery was.'

"That was the whole of it. Aunt Fran was asking *me* for forgiveness for the sins of the past generation! Then we had dinner together at Hilltop House, high up on the cliff, overlooking the valley where two rivers meet: the Shenandoah, which flows from south to north to join the Potomac, which flows southward. From Hilltop House we had a bird's-eye view of the valley where three states merge: Maryland of the Mason-Dixon line; Virginia of the South; the free state of West Virginia, which broke away from Virginia precisely over the issue of slavery."

It is for reasons like this moment of forgiveness sought and received that such historical shrines exist—so that we will not forget our past, murky though it may be; but rather that we may use our memories to heal the wounds of the past and build better futures.

Two years afterward my friend Sister Emma died as well; but like Emma, I will never forget the Harper's Ferry moment of grace when forgiveness reached out across generations to heal and reconcile. When we give and receive forgiveness, we discover that our bonds have been cut, the doors of our cages opened, and we are free to soar into God's distant and wondrous heights!

SIX FORGIVENESS-PRAYER TECHNIQUES

1. In your mind's eye bring yourself to the cross where Jesus is dying. Look up at Jesus, wounded as he is. Hold up to him your wounds, your hurts. See in your mind's eye the person or persons who have caused you these

hurts, coming also up the hill to the cross of Jesus. See him or her standing beside you. Give to Jesus the whole situation: your feelings, your anger, your wish to be forgiving, the difficulty you have in really forgiving. Ask Jesus for his forgiveness for yourself and for those who have hurt you. "Jesus, lend me *your* ability to forgive this person who has hurt me!" Reach out and take the person by the hand and lead him or her closer to the cross. Touch the cross. Hold on to it. See the other person touch it as well. Stay there with Jesus.

2. Read Luke 23:33–43. Read the passage slowly. There are two stories of forgiveness here. Using the method of *lectio divina*, stop reading when a phrase speaks to your heart. Reflect on the words. Let your heart respond to the words. Talk to Jesus from your heart about the passage; be open with your feelings—God understands. Then rest in the love of God as God's love envelops you.

3. Think of some of the people in your life whose actions or words have hurt you. As you visualize each one, say, "Jesus, forgive ———; he/she didn't know what he/she was doing."

4. Are there people in your life whom you have hurt? Is there a family misunderstanding in which you have taken one side and have, therefore, alienated other family members? In your mind's eye, come with all the members of this family feud to the cross of Jesus. Tell Jesus about the family argument from your point of view. Listen, in your imagination, as the other side of the family tells Jesus how they see the event, how they are hurt and why. Ask Jesus to step in and forgive and heal this family in ways you have no power to do. Ask

Jesus if there is anything you can do, any step you can take to make the situation better. If you receive guidance from the Holy Spirit, follow it through. You can repeat this prayer exercise as a regular, daily intercession for family healing. Be patient as the Holy Spirit gently works in the hearts of all those involved. Thank God for this healing of your family, which God is already in the process of bringing about.

5. A Prayer of Forgiveness:
    Dear God,
    My heart is heavy. I have been hurt again by ———.
    I surrender to you my feelings of deep hurt.
    Please help me to want to forgive.
    May your love be like a warm bath in which
        I can soak my heavy heart-pain.
    Help me to see the subconscious drives of ———
        that caused her/him to do what
        she/he did to me.
    Heal my perceptions so that I may be released
        from the bondage of my unforgiveness.
    In my pain and hurt, I pray that ——— be healed
        and that I may love her/him as you do.
    Forgive her/him; she/he did not know how
        she/he hurt me.
    Fill me with your own forgiving spirit, Jesus.

6. Pray the Prayer of Saint Francis:
    Loving God, make me a channel of your peace.
    Where there is hatred, let me sow love;
    Where there is injury, pardon;
    Where there is despair, hope;
    Where there is darkness, light;
    Where there is sadness, joy.

O Divine Master, grant that I may seek
Not so much to be consoled as to console;
To be understood as to understand;
To be loved as to love.
For it is in giving that we receive;
It is in pardoning that we are pardoned;
And it is in dying that we are born
    to eternal life.

7

TALK TO US, GOD

Regina

One evening last fall I had a phone call from my niece Sylvia. Her voice was anxious. "Aunt R., I don't know what to make of this. Sunday in church after Communion, God talked to me!…I know it wasn't me talking to myself…I heard the words in my head, but they weren't my words!…It was God talking!"

"And you're afraid you're weird or something?" I responded, detecting the frantic edge in her voice.

"Yes…I mean, does this happen to people, or am I going off the deep end?"

I assured Sylvia that she was not unbalanced and that this kind of spiritual experience *does* happen to people. "Yes, Sylvia, God does talk to people at times, just as you describe. What did God say?"

Sylvia explained how concerned she had been about a relational situation in her Episcopal church. As a member of the vestry, she had become acutely aware of a severe problem that seemed to endanger the harmony of parish life. She had prayed and prayed about it, storming heaven, beseeching God's help for the seemingly insoluble situation. Then on Sunday morning, as she prayed after holy Communion, she heard God say, "Be at peace! Don't worry about ———. I am taking care of it. All will be well!" Peace descended, and her heart was filled with an abiding wonder and joy—until, of course, she began to question the experience and ask herself if she were hallucinating.

This was a first-time event for her, and she was a recent Christian. "Am I loony?" she asked, "or does God really talk to people?"

She was greatly relieved when I told her that there are plenty of examples throughout Christian tradition, and she can read about them in the writings of the mystics. God had at times talked to me in much the same way, I also said "It's called a 'locution,'" I told her.

"Oh! Thank God, it has a name!—A locution!"

"This refers to the experience of God speaking to the external ear," I told her. "That is, one might hear God as you hear me talking to you now—or, as you experienced it, to the inner ear—the mind and heart. This is not surprising since God is so close and dear to us that God is *within* us and we are *within* God! We just don't realize this intimacy; and so, when God breaks the sound barrier and talks to us, we are surprised."

I told her that we can't control events like this. We cannot *make* them happen or force a repeat performance. God will talk to us when God wills, and when it does occur the proof of the reality for us is the fruit it bears. If it strengthens our prayer, fills us with joy and peace and gratitude, and gives us assurance of God's very special love for us, then the fruit of the moment of intimacy is good, and we may assume the experience is valid. Often, this graced moment comes when we are most desperately in need. It should not be dwelt upon. It does not mean we are "holier" than anyone else. To help us remain objective about our spiritual walk, it is advisable to have a mentor or spiritual adviser/friend with whom you can be open. A person who has experience in spiritual guidance and a knowledge of the Christian tradition can help us avoid pitfalls. I advised Sylvia to seek such a spiritual friend. For her, it turned out that her interim pastor was just such a person, well equipped both from life experience and from having taken the two-year program in spiritual direction offered by Shalem Spiritual Institute in Washington, D.C.

Spiritual writers in books on prayer narrate many ways God speaks to us: in Scripture, God's word; through the natural beauty of creation; through a phrase we come across in our reading that stops us in our tracks with its poignancy; through a homily we hear that seems to have been written specifically for us. Yet many people complain, "I pick up the Bible and read it, hoping God will speak to me like people say, but it's just confusing. I don't understand it, and I certainly don't hear God!"

To phrase it differently, then—does God speak to *everyone*, or is it just the favored few who can say, "God talks to me"? Why do some people who earnestly long for more intimacy with their God seem ungifted in this area?

First of all, I believe that God loves each person God has created with infinite tenderness. I believe God seeks a relationship with each of us. Therefore, I believe God speaks to everyone in one way or another at different points in their lives. What is unknown to me is what a *particular person* needs spiritually at any given moment, or what his or her expectations are regarding an intimate relationship, a *conversational* friendship with God. This kind of understanding is God's realm alone—the area of action of God's Holy Spirit.

Is this person who comes to me for counsel looking so hard for a profound experience that she misses God present in the ordinary and commonplace? Or does this person need some help in knowing how to sit with and savor the line of Scripture that warms the heart, because he yields to the impulse to cover a lot of ground by plowing ahead, page after page? Maybe this person needs to learn the discipline of *lectio divina*, the monastic way of listening to Scripture. I believe that God speaks and will speak to each of us in all the ways the spiritual books suggest as we are more attentive in our listening and more patient in our savoring.

When it happens, like the disciples on the Emmaus road, we will know we are hearing God in the scriptural passage, in the sunset, in the undulating mountains, in the Sunday homily, in the word of a friend that takes our breath away in one of those "aha" moments, because our hearts will burn within us!

I shared with Sylvia a couple of personal stories of God's intervention so that she would feel more at ease with her experience.

In 1972 I was recovering from surgery in the Sisters' infirmary near Philadelphia. I was in charge of the drama department at Little Flower High School in North Philadelphia, and in the spring of each year the selection of a major musical for the following fall had to be made. In prayer I heard God say to me, "The next production at Little Flower will be your last."

"Well then, God," I replied. "I choose *Fiddler on the Roof* because of what it says about the intimate way we can talk with you. If I am to make one last statement, that is what I would like to say—that we can talk to you the way Tevye does, as a friend."

The choice of production was not totally up to me: the idea had to be approved by both principal and music director—no small hurdle to leap! They did agree, however, and *Fiddler* was a wonderful learning and community-building experience for all of us. We taught ourselves the technical aspects of creating side stages with backlighting; we mastered mime techniques for several sequences; and we learned about Judaism from a rabbi who served as consultant. But also, God spoke to me in a different way, although no less clearly than before.

I had been frantically looking for a "Tevye cart"—something rustic with two wheels that Tevye could pull or push onto our very small stage—one that could pass as authentic for a milk-vender's vehicle. In every antique shop or junk store we passed all summer long, in our trips upstate and down, I had my eyes peeled for just such a Tevye cart. No luck! We went into production in September with Tevye miming a cart. This was *not good!* We needed the real thing, and I was bombarding God about the prop! Then one day my stage manager, Bob Hampson, came bursting into rehearsal. He had found just the thing, *only three blocks away from the school!* A man had several of them that he rented out to the paper pickers—the people who collected papers, aluminum cans, and rags, which they could turn into hard cash at certain centers. He would rent us one for fifteen dollars a week! This time God spoke to me *in the event!* The message was "The thing you need is always close at hand!"

This proved true again when, for the same production,

we needed *wooden* buckets. Nowhere could they be found. In desperation I sent two of the stage crew to the local Ben Franklin store to buy wood-facsimile contact paper. "We'll have to doctor up metal buckets," I said in disgust, "but as sure as anything one will tip over during a performance and *sound* like a metal bucket. I hate that! It's very poor theater!"

Off the girls went, and when they discovered that Ben Franklin had no wood-grained contact paper, they crossed the street to the hardware store. The owner asked what they wanted the paper for, and when they told him, he replied, "But girls, I have *wooden* buckets." From his storeroom he produced two perfect wooden buckets! Again I got the message loud and clear: "What you need is *always* close at hand!"

Ever since that day I don't look far and wide for whatever is my current need. I know God will supply, and it's *always right in front of my nose!*

Yes, *Fiddler* was my last production at Little Flower High School—my last *full* production, that is. A year later I was again in the infirmary, recovering from another surgery. This time, out of the blue, came the words "There will be a change in the direction of your life; but do not be afraid. I will take care of it when the time comes."

"Oh, thank you, God!" was all I could say. But it was time to select another major production, so I chose *Hello, Dolly*. I didn't get to finish it, however. *Fiddler* was my last completed production! In late August, on a trip to a theater conference in Washington, D.C., I found my Aunt Olive dying; and my cousin, who totally depended on her as a physically challenged young woman, was in need of help. This necessitated many trips to Washington, wedged in between classroom teaching and rehearsals. By October it was clear to me, my spiritual director, and my superiors that my health would break if something were not done. Within two weeks I was transferred to Virginia to do a totally different ministry—to attend to my cousin's rehabilitation. This was quite a "change of direction"!

"OK, God," I challenged. "When something is of your will, you always tie up the loose ends. We need a director to bring *Hello, Dolly* through dress rehearsal to final production within two weeks!"

Again, Bob Hampson appeared with a piece of good news. A LaSalle University student whose one-act play I had admired in a contest setting had just graduated in June. He was free, and the last production he had directed was (you guessed it!) *Hello, Dolly*! He came to Little Flower, we overlapped efforts for a week, the students were relieved to see how smoothly things were going; and when I left, he completed the show!

God had spoken again, but in action, not in words. God had supplied the need, and verified for me that I was still moving in God's plan and will.

A few weeks ago I met Carol Williams, who took a big step in faith in opening her own family restaurant where she and her son and daughters all work. As with any new business, this one involved a large capital investment, and the anxiety of making ends meet is always hovering. As bills piled up, her stress was mounting, and one day Carol was in a severe depression. As she drove her car along the causeway that leads from mainland Virginia onto Chincoteague Island where her new restaurant is located, she felt a strong urge to end her stress by driving over the embankment. She fought the emotion, gritted her teeth, maneuvered the causeway, and pulled up in front of Castaways, her restaurant, on Maddox Boulevard. When she entered the restaurant she saw, shining forth from the room-sized mirror on the wall of the back dining area, a radiant cross. It took her breath away because, without words, she knew God was saying to her, "Don't be discouraged. I am taking care of you!"

Carol called out, and other members of her family hurried to her side. They also saw the glowing cross. Her son searched for an explanation—for something, anything that could be causing a cross-shaped reflection in the mirror, but he could find nothing. The cross remained for about twenty minutes, then faded and was gone; but Carol's heart is warmed by her message from God. Her depression has lifted, her confidence is restored.

My friend, David Welsh, was experiencing strange dizzy spells that were of serious concern to him and his wife, Kay. One Saturday we were sitting together at Mass in St. Andrew Church on Chincoteague Island. It was the Christmas season, and on the wall directly in front of us was a large painting of the Madonna and Child. As David looked at the picture he heard a woman's voice say to him, "Don't be afraid. You are healed!" Thinking I might have spoken to him, he looked at me questioningly. Later, Kay explained to me what had happened. David kept all medical appointments, but the spells of dizziness had ceased. The experience has deeply affected him and changed his life.

So, yes, I am suggesting that intimate communication between God, God's saints, and human beings *is* experienced, or is *meant to be* experienced, by *everyone!* Of course, there are no statistics about this, but as I minister pastorally and listen to people's stories, I discover more and more people are hearing God's voice in one way or another. Neither I nor my niece nor my restaurant-owner friend nor my friend David are unique in this. God's love embraces and holds in existence each one of us. Each person may rightly say, "I am singularly loved by God who dwells within me!" Communication comes when we are most needy, most broken, and, therefore, most open to God's intervention. This talking to and hearing God intensifies and personalizes our experience of God-presence, builds our confidence, and enables us to take the next step in faith. This kind of graced moment confirms our trust that our God is always ready to unite God-self with each of us. Like the tenderest parent, God cherishes us!

On the other hand, it is possible to silence God's voice speaking to us. For me, there was a period of several years when I became afraid and turned away from this intimacy. Like my niece Sylvia, I was afraid that I was "losing it" and slipping into self-deception. I was also afraid that as I was moved to yield more and more of myself to God's action, I would change—I would no longer be *me*—I would lose control! Basically, I said to God, "Hold off, God! Not so fast! Let me catch my breath. Let me just stay here—this is far enough for awhile." God respects our wills, and so, for a long time, the intimacy of a communicating friendship was quiet. I share this not because my choice to go with my fear was right. I know I was lacking in trust; and I also know that fear has no place in the heart of a child of God. I think I was selfishly clinging to a plateau instead of moving ahead spiritually on the upward climb. God, however, while respecting my choice of spiritual lethargy, never stopped loving me! *God never stops loving us.* And to return to God is as simple as turning around and reaching out one's hand, as easy as replacing a frown with a smile.

Once, some years back, during a retreat, God let me know that my "pet name" is *Shama*—Listener. I am again trying to be that listener, ready to hear whatever God may speak. May we all grow as listeners to God in the many commonplace ways God speaks to us. Each time we hear God's voice, let our hearts rejoice that we are invited into conversation with the Creator of the Universe, because God has made human beings the epitome of creation, in God's own image, and has called us his *friends!*

PRAYER WAYS FOR WOULD-BE "LISTENERS"

Listening to God in Scripture

Use *lectio divina* twice a day for fifteen to thirty minutes. This method of praying the Scripture has been used in Benedictine and Cistercian monasteries for centuries as a means of opening mind and heart to contemplation. Today, more and more laypeople are using *lectio* as a lead into centering prayer.

Lectio—Read

Read a portion of Scripture. Try the Gospel of John, chapter 14 as a beginning. This is Christ's Last Supper message. Do not try to read all of chapter 14— just read the words of Jesus reverently and slowly. When a word or phrase stands out and touches your heart, *linger there!*

Reflect

Think about the meaning of this passage to you, now. Why did it have a special appeal for you? What is God inviting you to in these words?

Pray

Talk to Jesus from your heart. This prayer will flow automatically as you reflect. Words may well up within you; praise and gratitude to God may spill over the edges of your inner joy. This should lead you to…

Contemplate

…in rapt silence the presence of God in which you should simply rest.

Come gently back to an awareness of the daily life that surrounds you. This portion of the *lectio* prayer is being called in today's parlance "centering prayer."

Quieting Prayer

As you read your Bible, see if there are not lines of Scripture that bring a sense of peace over you. Examples might be "Come to me, all you who labor and carry heavy burdens, and I will give you rest" (Matthew 11:28 *Inclusive New Testament*); "I am gentle and humble of heart, and you will find rest for your soul" (Matthew 11:29 *Inclusive*

New Testament); "In God's house there are many dwelling places…I am indeed going to prepare a place for you" (John 14:2–3 *Inclusive New Testament*); "Do not be afraid, little flock; for it is your Father's good pleasure to give you the kingdom" (Luke 12:32 *New Revised Standard Version Bible*). Enjoy that sense of peace for a few moments.

Recalling Peace-Giving Prayers

Find lines from favorite prayers or from the sayings of the saints that give you peace and courage. Memorize and use them the same way. Two of my favorites are the following:

From Saint Teresa of Avila:

Let nothing disturb you:
Let nothing afright you;
All things are passing:
Only God is changeless.
Who has God wants for nothing.
God alone suffices!

From Saint Julian of Norwich:

All shall be well, and all shall be well, and all manner of thing shall be well.

In God's Presence
(which, you recall, is always where you already are!)

Ask God to make of you a good "listener." Think of the things in your day today that have spoken to you of God's love. Name them, and thank God for using them as God's mouthpieces to you.

Walk in the Beauty of Nature

Take a nature walk, specifically to hear sounds that speak to you of God's love. After you have done this, begin to concentrate on things you *see* that tell of God's love. You can do this exercise with each of your senses (although you may fare better using your sense of taste on returning home, *in your own kitchen*). Spend a few minutes in praise of God for speaking to you through nature.

Practice Friend-Sharing

If you have a friend with whom you can share your thoughts about God, share with your friend how you are trying to be aware of the many ways God speaks to you of God's love. Listen to your friend when he or she shares personal experiences. If you are comfortable doing it, pray together a prayer of thanks. If you are uncomfortable with spontaneous prayer, pray a prayer from the tradition: the Lord's Prayer or the Glory Be.

Keep a Spiritual Journal

Take time each day to note the way in which you are listening to the signs of God's love. Write down your efforts and experiences. Thank God for these graces.

8

FEAR NOT,
TRUST ALWAYS

Regina

The Scriptures are full of the calming words *Do not be afraid! Do not be anxious! Be at peace! Trust God!* There must be a reason for the repeated admonition *Fear not!* If you have ever been paralyzed by fear, you can easily understand why it is necessary for God to put us at ease and free us from the fears that bind us. Fear holds us down. Anxiety makes us incapable of action. To enable us to move on and take the next step, God allays our fears.

In your teenage years did you ever take a "trust walk"? It is one of the rituals used in youth groups as a community-building activity to help new members discover that their fellow members care and can be trusted. The participants are blindfolded and entrust themselves to the guidance of an older member to be led safely to the designated meeting place. God has been leading us on such a trust walk. The future is uncertain. The destination is often uncertain. But God lets us feel sufficiently the touch of a guiding hand that we have the courage to move on.

Once fear has evaporated, we can begin to trust another.

Each successful step forward as our trust is rewarded enables us to dare more, to trust more easily, and to take the next step forward.

I once had a dream in which I was walking with God, who was a quiet Radiance behind me, as I moved along a dark stone walkway. The problem was, I didn't know where I was headed, or how long it would take to get there; and there was only enough light from this Radiant Presence to uncover the next steppingstone. But the presence was calming, and though everything about the trip was shrouded in uncertainty, I was able to take the next step because of the light on the pathway. Each time I did so, the light exposed the next stone, and I could trust enough to step on that exposed stone.

God's support is like that. My subconscious was affirming my trust mode! God delights in allaying our fears enough so that we can take the next step. In this way our *trust* in God builds through the very exercise of trust. This is the spiritual calisthenic we need to build trust muscle! It is much like the *manna* experience of the Israelites during the forty years in the desert. Each day they would gather the manna bread that had appeared on the grass during the night, but *only enough for the day.* They could not gather two days' supply, so as to save the effort of going back to gather tomorrow! Of course, they tried it! That is human nature—to find a "new way," a "better way," "our own way"! When the Israelites experimented with gathering a second day's supply of manna, they found the time wasted, because the manna rotted and was inedible.

God seems to want from us this kind of walking in faith or trust, that if God supplies our manna (whatever is our need *today*), God will provide tomorrow's as well.

In 1978 I was in the state of being "in between." I was on leave of absence from the religious community of which I had been a member for twenty-four years, involved in caring for the needs and rehabilitation of my cousin. I had been advised by my spiritual director and by the vicar that I would probably not be able to return with peace of mind to my religious community, and that it was time for some in-depth discernment of God's will regarding my future. Sister Bridget, my friend during this dark time, was living under the same uncertainty. We began to pray together: "God, here we are; what would you have us do?" In those days, the triumphant song that had recently come out of the Charismatic Renewal gave us encouragement: "Trust in the Lord; you shall not tire. Serve the Lord; you shall not weaken; for the Lord's own strength will uphold you! You shall renew your life, and live!" The rousing beat of the music and the strength of the lyrics seemed to inundate us with enough courage for the next step.

It was at this time that I remember feeling as if I were being challenged to walk on water. That is how uncertain everything seemed. So much so that I wrote the childlike song "Walk on the Water with Me." The simple lyrics go, "Walk on the water with me! Walk on the water with me! Peter, step out of the boat and walk on the water with me." When this chorus is repeated, instead of "Peter," one inserts his or her own name.

The discernment process for both of us led us *out* of the tried and familiar, out of our former religious community, but, for awhile, toward and not yet *into* a discernible future. We continued the waiting prayer—what do You want us to do?—and the water-walk, one step at a time. Today, we can look back and see that every minute of the way we were never alone. Today, we can be grateful to God for having challenged us. We have had new beginnings more than once and find ourselves among Sisters with a fresh and daring vision, Sisters for Christian Community. While remaining open to what the Holy Spirit is bringing about in us and not being so eager for security that we define this prematurely, we Sisters are getting on with the mission of ministry to God's people in any and all ways service is needed.

We are not alone in finding ourselves "in between." That is why I share this part of my story. There are people out there in today's world who find themselves in similar crises: between jobs, after broken relationships, uncertain of medical outcomes. The "in betweens" are many and varied, but each one can seem a very scary place to be. To move from standstill to progress, however, we need to be released from the "scars," at least enough to move in the direction indicated by circumstances. For those who know God, *nothing* is ever just "circumstance" or "chance," unless you say "graced circumstance," "blessed chance!" As we come to trust God's presence in the journey, the puzzle pieces of life begin to come together in recognizable picture parts. At the end of life we shall undoubtedly be allowed to see the entire panorama of our lives and rejoice with the God who was and is always present to us, even in the midst of crisis.

PRAYER WAYS TO BANISH FEAR AND GROW IN TRUST

Use Musical Therapy

Find a song that verbalizes for you the trust in God you so badly need and the banishing of fear. For you, it may be the popular hymn-song "Be Not Afraid." For me it was "Trust in the Lord, You Shall Not Tire" and my own little jingle "Walk on the Water with Me." Someone may get courage from the more secular "Whenever I Feel Afraid" ("I hold my head erect, and whistle a happy tune, so no one will suspect I'm afraid!"). The musical vamp in the song contains the lovely twist "For when I fool the people, you see, I fool myself as well!" Play this music in your car, on your tape recorder first thing in the morning, on your walkman, over and over as often as you need it to soothe your soul. When you are mentally singing the words, you are, after all, praying! Did you ever think of that before?

Recall Life's Little Triumphs

Reflect on the triumphs of your life, the ones you have already lived through—little triumphs or big ones. As you recall each one of these, make it part of your personal litany of thanks!

Nourish Yourself with Scriptural "Fear Nots"

Some of these scriptural admonitions may be just what you need today. Choose one for your reflection and spend a few minutes with it. You might stop periodically, as you do for a coffee break, and say it to yourself again. If none of the following seems right for you, look in your New Testament for one that speaks to your need. The following quotations from the *New Revised Standard Version Bible* are only a sampling:

"Joseph, son of David, do not be afraid to take Mary as your wife" (Matthew 1:20).

When Zechariah saw [the angel], he was terrified and fear overwhelmed him. But the angel said to him, "Do not be afraid, Zechariah, for your prayer has been heard" (Luke 1:12–13).

The angel said to Mary, "Do not be afraid, Mary; for you have been favored by God. And now you will conceive…and bear a son, and you will name him 'Jesus'" (Luke 1:30–31).

An angel of the Lord stood before them [the shepherds], and the glory of the Lord shone around them, and they were terrified. But the angel said to them: "Do not be afraid—I am bringing you good news of great joy!" (Luke 2:9–10).

Someone came from the leader's [Jairus'] house saying: "Your daughter is dead." "…Only believe and she will be saved" (Luke 8:49–50).

"Do not worry about your life, what you will eat, or about your body, what you will wear….Consider the ravens, they neither sow nor reap…and yet,

God feeds them. Of how much more value are you?" (Luke 12:22, 24).

"Do not be afraid, little flock, for it is your Father's good pleasure to give you the kingdom" (Luke 12:32).

Jesus stood among them and said to them, "Peace be with you....Why are you frightened...? Look at my hands and my feet, and see that it is myself" (Luke 24:36, 38–39).

When they saw Jesus walking on the sea...they were terrified. But he said to them, "It is I; do not be afraid" (John 6:19–20).

"Do not let your hearts be troubled! Believe in God; believe also in me" (John 14:1).

"Peace I leave with you; my peace I give to you.... Do not let your hearts be troubled, and do not let them be afraid" (John 14:27).

"As the Father has loved me, so I have loved you; abide in my love" (John 15:9).

Look into the Hebrew Scriptures

Here are some texts from the *New Revised Standard Version Bible* that may stimulate you to experience God's peace. Use them as you did those from the New Testament, and look for others in your Bible. You will be astonished to see how often the Scriptures urge us to put aside fear and trust God.

> Trust in God and God will help you; make your ways straight, and hope in God (Sirach 2:6).

> I will remove disaster from you so that you will not bear reproach and I will deal with all your oppressors....I will save the lame and gather the outcast, and I will change their shame into praise....At that time I will bring you home (Zephaniah 3:18–20).

> I have loved you with an everlasting love: therefore I have continued my faithfulness to you (Jeremiah 31:3).

> "Do not be afraid of them, for I am with you to deliver you, says the Lord" (Jeremiah 1:8).

> Do not fear, for you will not be ashamed. Do not be discouraged, for you will not suffer disgrace....For your Maker is your husband, the Lord of hosts is God's name, the Holy One of Israel is your Redeemer (Isaiah 54:4–5).

> I am God who comforts you; why then are you afraid of a mere mortal who must die, a human being who fades like grass? (Isaiah 51:12).

> Surely God is my salvation: I will trust, and will not be afraid, for the Lord God is my strength and my might; God has become my salvation (Isaiah 12:2).

Trust in the Lord with all your heart, and do not rely on your own insight. In all your ways acknowledge God, and God will make straight your paths (Proverbs 3:5–6).

As a mother comforts her child, so will I comfort you; in Jerusalem you shall find your comfort (Isaiah 66:13).

Pray Psalm 136

How often will one of the psalms say for us just what we are feeling? In our century we are sometimes unwilling to say to God, outright, what we are honestly feeling and thinking. If I am really upset and frustrated, I may restrain myself from total honesty in my prayer with the idea that I should only say "nice things" to God. No, prayer is honest conversation, from the heart. God wants to hear from us exactly what the hurt is all about. Even if I am angry at God, I can express that honestly. I expressed it to my parents often enough. God is my unconditionally loving parent! Psalm 136 reminds us over and over that "God's steadfast love endures forever." After you read the psalmist's version, you might write your own, using your personal life experiences but keeping the refrain: "God's steadfast love endures forever."

9

SHARE WITH SOUL SISTERS

Bridget

There is a feeling in the air now, a connection, an energy that is bringing women together from different generations, cultures, ethnic groups, and religions around the world. Conferences such as the global gathering of women that took place in Beijing in 1995 continue to create ripples of hope for transformation for women in our society who dream of a new world in which there is peace and justice for people everywhere.

I experience this same intuitive sense of women-power on *Godtalk*, a new program that I produce and host that airs on cable TV. In a recent series, "Women of Faith," women scholars from the Jewish, Muslim, and Christian traditions shared their perspectives on women in the Bible. As we dialogued, it became apparent that women from different backgrounds were exploring new pathways to healing and peace. We were able to relinquish our agendas and discover common ground. On one such program, a Muslim woman explained that Sarah, the Jewish matriarch, is revered in her tradition. The Jewish rabbi recalled the "bad rap" the Jewish rabbis who authored the midrash had given to Hagar. The African-American theologian discussed Hagar from the perspective of the black experience of oppression and empowerment. It occurred to me that here we were naming and confronting the biases that have kept religions apart for centuries. We were getting rid of misinformation and discussing new meanings that would enable these biblical women to mentor us in our spiritual journeys. We were discovering common ground. We were opening ourselves up to the Spirit in our midst.

Like the women scholars on *Godtalk,* women and men today can find spiritual enrichment in encountering biblical women such as Ruth and Naomi, Elizabeth and Mary, the Mother of Jesus, and Martha and Mary. These sisters of the faith can be role models for us as we strive to live the gospel in our times. Let us take a glimpse at a few of the stories of vibrant, human women who opened their hearts to other women as companions, friends, and soul sisters.

In the Hebrew Scripture's Book of Ruth, we meet Ruth and her mother-in-law, Naomi. Ruth left her homeland in Moab and accompanied Naomi to Bethlehem after the deaths of Naomi's husband and sons. Upon her arrival, Ruth went to work, harvesting crops in the fields, to support Naomi. Here she met Boaz, a relative of Naomi. Naomi engaged in some clever matchmaking to bring Boaz and Ruth together. Ruth followed the advice of her mother-in-law, married Boaz, and gave birth to Obed, the grandfather of King David.

In this story Ruth is praised for her faithful love and loyalty to Naomi. She refused to return to her homeland and vowed to follow Naomi wherever she went. Ruth proclaimed her deep affection for her mother-in-law: "Do not press me to leave you or to turn back from following you!

Where you go, I will go; where you lodge, I will lodge; your people shall be my people, and your God my God. Where you die, I will die—there will I be buried" (Ruth 1:16–17 *New Revised Standard Version Bible*). There is no other example of friendship between human beings like Ruth's promise to Naomi anywhere else in the Bible. This is even more remarkable because Ruth was a foreigner, an outsider who left her family, religion, and culture to be a companion to Naomi. By taking this step, Ruth risked poverty, rejection, and ridicule. Yet, in a reversal, which scholars believe is a critique of Israel's ruling elite who excluded foreigners from their society, the biblical writers described Ruth as the heroine of the story.

Naomi was the ideal mother-in-law who looked out for Ruth's best interest. She guided Ruth into Boaz's embrace. According to the text, Naomi treated Ruth's baby like her own child. She nursed him, and her neighbors remarked that Ruth was of greater value to Naomi than seven sons—the ultimate compliment in this culture. How's that for gratitude!

Ruth and Naomi were two women who shared much of life's joy and sorrow. They were married, widowed, had children, and lived in exile in a foreign land. They helped each other. They had the kind of friendship that some women today experience and others seek. They were survivors in a society that marginalized them. Nonwhite women from different cultures, ethnic backgrounds, and religions today can relate to their survival skills. Like Ruth, God chooses the outsiders, the foreigners, or the marginalized in a society to be the models of God's inclusive love for all people everywhere. The story of Ruth and Naomi offers a powerful message that love can transform us and make a difference in our world. We do not need to allow our prejudices or biases to destroy us; rather, we can commit ourselves to lend a helping hand and a listening ear to those in need wherever we may find them. Sometimes, like Ruth and Naomi, we need look no further than our own families.

According to the Gospel of Luke, Mary and Elizabeth were relatives and confidants who shared their innermost thoughts and feelings with each other. The angel appeared to Mary and announced her miraculous conception of Emmanuel—"God with us"—then told her the good news about Elizabeth: "And now, your relative Elizabeth in her old age has also conceived a son; and this is the sixth month for her who was said to be barren. For nothing will be impossible with God" (1:36–37 *New Revised Standard Version Bible*). As soon as Mary found out that Elizabeth was pregnant, she immediately dashed off to Elizabeth and Zachary's home for a three-month visit. I cannot help wondering if Mary had morning sickness when she undertook this arduous journey and if Elizabeth had a difficult pregnancy. One thing we know for sure is that they were both pregnant by divine intervention. Elizabeth was beyond menopause and had known infertility for many years. Mary, on the other hand, was young, fertile, but a virgin.

The moment Mary greeted her, Elizabeth's baby danced for joy in her womb. Filled with the Holy Spirit, Elizabeth affirmed Mary's motherhood. She recognized that her relative was carrying the body and blood of Christ within her. "Blessed are you among women, and blessed is the fruit of your womb. And why has this happened to me that the mother of my God comes to me? For as soon as I heard the sound of your greeting, the child in my womb leaped for joy" (1:42–44 *New Revised Standard Version Bible*).

Then Mary shared the depths of her gratitude with her wise mentor in the canticle of praise known as the Magnificat. Mary expressed in this prayer her profound experience of God's liberating love in her life and proclaimed the divine tender mercies that raise up the oppressed and poor and knock down the proud and arrogant.

This encounter between a young woman and an old woman—between two pregnant women—reflects the hopes and dreams of women through the ages who are filled with the life-giving power of God. Christians today are challenged to be like Mary and Elizabeth, the Body of Christ birthing the life-giving power of God in the world. Like Mary, we can use our gifts to companion others in need; and like Elizabeth, we can recognize and affirm the Christ within others around us and everywhere. Mary and Elizabeth are visible reminders that women can celebrate their identity because God continues to leap in wombs, touch hearts, and transform lives since God is in us and of us. Like Mary and Elizabeth, women today reflect the feminine face of God in our world.

As sure as Mary gave birth to God in human flesh, Christians can give birth to God over and over through acts of loving kindness to friends and strangers alike. All we have to do is embrace one another in genuine love, like our soul sisters Mary and Elizabeth. The Holy Spirit will do the rest, if we open our hearts, serve others, and sing God's praises.

No reflection on women's relationships in the Bible would be complete without a look at two of the most famous sisters in history—Mary and Martha. According to the story, Jesus is a guest in their home. Martha is busy preparing the meal, and Mary is relaxing in Jesus' presence, listening to his words. Right away, Martha bursts on the scene to complain about Mary's lack of helpfulness in preparing the meal: "Do you not care that my sister has left me to do all the work by myself? Tell her then to help me" (Luke 10:40 *New Revised Standard Version Bible*).

At first glance, Mary and Martha appear to be competitive sisters in conflict over their different agendas. Martha seems to be a nag who is at her wit's end with her sister's behavior, and Mary seems to be a bit withdrawn. But if we take another look, we see that Martha is a woman who gets things done. She is competent and unafraid to challenge her close friend Jesus. According to the Gospel of John, Jesus loves Martha and reveals to her one of the most important messages in the history of Christianity—the meaning of the Resurrection. Martha's confession of Christ is similar to Peter's confession. According to the narrative, Jesus said to Martha, "I am the resurrection and the life. Those who believe in me, even though they die, will live, and everyone who lives and believes in me will never die. Do you believe this?" Martha replies, "Yes, Lord, I believe that you are the Messiah, the Son of God, the one coming into the world" (John 11:25–27 *New Revised Standard Version Bible*).

Now back to the supper scene. In his response to Martha's complaint about her sister, Jesus affirms women's value. In a society that placed little worth in women and viewed them as the property of men, Jesus asserts the rights of women to be disciples and equals with men. He affirms Mary as a learner and a disciple: "Martha, Martha, you are worried and distracted over many things, there is need of only one thing. Mary has chosen the better part, which will not be taken away from her" (Luke 10:41–42 *New Revised Standard Version Bible*).

When we feel envious or competitive with other women, perhaps we can find a clue to these drives in our driven "Martha"-like tendencies or our passive-aggressive "Mary" side. Or we could ask ourselves if we are adopting a male model of hierarchical values in our relationships with others. Elisabeth Schussler Fiorenza believes that Jesus' rebuke to Martha is a reflection of the patriarchal Church's attempt to keep women in a subordinate position (*In Memory of Her*, 165). Perhaps, as this renowned scholar suggests, Martha is a symbol of eucharistic ministry.

Today, contemporary women often face conflicts between their roles as caregivers and their roles as career professionals. Most women I know either feel guilty about their choice or exhaust themselves trying to do it all. Like Martha, we need to nurture the physical needs of our spouses, children, and older parents. Like Mary, we need to care for all their spiritual needs. But like Martha, we need also to care for our own physical needs, and like Mary, we need to tend to our own spiritual hungers. The question often arises *How can we be both Martha and Mary? Can we have it all, or do we need to choose?* There are no easy answers to these dilemmas. However, no matter what our choice, we can focus on the one necessary thing of which Jesus reminds us. We can live the liberating message of Jesus as disciples and equals. When we do this, we'll be able to affirm both the "Mary" and "Martha" in ourselves—no longer in competition but in harmony—showing us the way to wholeness and peace in our lives. We will be sisters and friends at last.

The stories of women in Scripture affect the way women

think and feel about themselves. They remind us of our inner truths and struggles to live the gospel as faithful witnesses to Jesus' liberating presence in ambiguous times. They call us to live in solidarity with them as guides and soul mates—companions on the journey dwelling in God, working for justice and full of love for everyone and everything. What a treasure chest of womanspirit we have in our biblical sisters! Their witness energizes our hopes and dreams that the vision in the heart of Jesus—that all may be one—will become a reality in our times.

PRAYER EXPERIENCE:
SHARE WITH SOUL SISTERS

Guided Prayer Encounter with Ruth and Naomi

Relax your body by releasing any stress you feel in your muscles....Start at the top of your head and proceed to the soles of your feet, alternately tightening and relaxing the muscles in each area of your body....Breathe deeply from the diaphragm....Feel the air as it moves in and out of your nostrils.... Imagine God breathing love, energy, peace, and joy into your body, mind, and spirit....Be aware that God is giving you whatever you most need right now....

Read the story of Ruth and Naomi in the Book of Ruth....

Conduct a mental conversation or write a letter to Ruth and/or Naomi, expressing your thoughts, insights, and feelings….

Invite Ruth and/or Naomi into your life for a day…. Let them accompany you through your activities, meet your family, friends….Sit down for a cup of tea or coffee and share with them your goals and challenges to live as a person of integrity and faith in our society….

Reflect on the marginalized, the outsiders, the foreigners, the people who are rejected or oppressed in our society….Ask Ruth and/or Naomi for ways you can reach out to them….

Share your close relationships with your biblical sisters….Name the gifts you have given and received from your women friends….

Choose one friendship to focus on now….Become aware of ways you experienced God's loving presence in your life through this special relationship…. Give thanks for this friend….Imagine Ruth and/or Naomi, your friend, and yourself in a circle of women, telling stories about faithful love and devoted friendship that nurture our womanspirits….

Be still and take this experience into the depths of your heart….Simply be with your close companions in God's Spirit….

Imagine a way to celebrate your close women relationships, such as sharing a meal, a phone call, a letter that expresses your appreciation for the gift of shared mutual love....

Encounter the "Mary and Martha" within You

In the stillness, open yourself to God's peace, harmony, joy, and love....If negative thoughts arise, simply let them float away as logs float down a river....Repeat the words *peace, harmony, joy,* or *love* slowly....As you do so, image God's loving presence filling your mind, body, and spirit....

See yourself in a place of natural beauty....Let the Earth speak to you....Be attentive to flowers, plants, animals, trees, sky—all that you can see, hear, taste, touch, smell around you....Everywhere you turn, God is speaking to you about your connection with your environment....Write down your thoughts and feelings about the goodness of the Earth....

Reflect on God's acceptance of you as you are.... Name your strengths and gifts....Name your weaknesses and wounds....Ask God to help you see yourself as God does....

Be aware of your "Mary" side (the contemplative/ student) and your "Martha" side (the activist/ achiever)....

Make a list of your gifts from each aspect of your personality....Write next to each what each gift has meant to you and to family, friends, neighbors, strangers, community, church, earth, world....

Reflect on ways you have developed your inner self and reached out in service in the last year....Be aware of the people who have encouraged your growth....Who are the people who have shaped your values? What struggles did you experience between your "Mary" and "Martha" sides, your contemplative and activist sides, your nurturing of self and others, your caregiving role and your career? What risks did you take? What connections did you make? Be conscious of the Spirit's surprises that made you more aware of your need for balance and harmony in your life....How can you reconcile these two different dimensions of your personality?...Write down your thoughts and feelings, insights, dreams about each of these encounters....

Be aware of opportunities for greater freedom and deeper love in your life....Are you willing to make the changes necessary for transformation to happen? for balance and harmony to occur? Write down your responses....

Be aware that God loves you in your imbalances and struggles....No one has it all together.... Imagine God embracing you with all your questions and shortcomings and ambiguities....Invite God to speak to your heart....Feel God's passionate love for you....Dialogue with God about the immeasurable depths of Divine Love for you as you are right now....

Play some of your favorite music. Paint, sculpt, sing, dance, or find some other way to celebrate your spiritual growth in the "Mary" and "Martha" aspects of your life....Invite others to celebrate a time of growth, risk-taking, new beginning—a life-giving experience in the "Mary and Martha" dimensions of your personality....Journal your thoughts and feelings about this sharing....

Guided Prayer Experience with Mary the Mother of Jesus

Compose your own canticle of praise or "Magnificat" for the gifts of God's loving tenderness in your life, or pray with Mary the following canticle:

My soul proclaims your goodness, O God,
and my spirit rejoices in you, my Savior.
For you have looked with favor
upon your lowly servant,
from this day forward
all generations will call me blessed.
For you, the Almighty, you have done great things
    for me,
and holy is your Name.
Your mercy reaches from age to age
for those who fear you.
You have shown strength with your arm,

you have scattered the proud in their conceit,
you have deposed the mighty from their thrones
and raised the lowly to high places.
You have filled the hungry with good things,
while you have sent the rich away empty.
You have come to the aid of Israel your servant,
mindful of your mercy—
the promise you made to our ancestors—to Sarah
    and Abraham
and their descendants forever (Luke 1:46–55 *In-
    clusive New Testament*).

Epilogue

EXTRA PRAYER EXPERIENCES

The following prayer experiences provide additional ways you can discover a glimpse into God's love in your life. They are meant to be savored and sampled as "delicious tastes" of divinity everywhere you turn.

THE PRAYER OF OPEN HANDS

Be still and quiet. Breathe in and out slowly.

In your imagination, be aware of the people you love....Let each one come to mind....Look into their eyes and share your feelings of warmth and love with them....Be aware of any areas of concern you have....Share these areas with them....

Open your hands and surrender your close relationships one by one to God....Ask God to bless each person....

Be aware of any blockages in letting go and giving everyone you love to God....

Be conscious of your feelings. Are you joyful? anxious? sad? afraid? peaceful?...

Share these feelings with God....

Express your appreciation for each relationship....

A PRAYER OF GRATITUDE FOR LIFE

Use the following as prayer starters, or compose your own prayers of gratitude for life.

I thank you, God, for this day because....

I thank you, God, for tall trees that sway to the breath of Divine Love in a gentle breeze....

I thank you, God, for sunny blue skies that radiate your shimmering, sparkling light....

I thank you, God, for furry creatures to caress and hold....

I thank you, God, for red and yellow tulips that grow in my spring garden....

I thank you, God, for snowflakes that cover the earth in a wholly white blanket on a winter's morn....

I thank you, God, for green grass that tickles my toes as I stroll on a summer's day....

I thank you, God, for the clear, cool water that refreshes my body and soul....

I thank you, God, for my family....

I thank you, God, for my friends....

I thank you, God, for my health....

I thank you, God, for my body and mind....

I thank you, God, for my faith....

A PRAYER OF OPENING TO HEALING AND TRANSFORMATION

In this prayer, listen as God speaks healing words to your heart!

My love is like a wave breaking on the shore of eternity, forever washing over your weaknesses and wounds.

My mercy endures forever. Every time you fail, I will forgive and will heal you.

Alone you can do nothing. With me you can do everything.

Let my grace transform you and heal your heart.

Know that I make everything work together for the good of those who love me.

I can transform even your weaknesses and failures into blessings if you allow me.

Believe that you are filled with the healing presence of my Spirit.

Enter into my heart of divine compassion and let my love light a healing fire within your soul.

I release my power in your life now, and you will continue to grow in the depths and heights of my love.

Be at peace, my beloved. I am the God who dwells within you and embraces you with tenderness forever.

ABOUT THE AUTHORS

R egina Madonna Oliver, SFCC, is also known by her given name as Loris Lee Oliver. She holds a master's degree from Marquette University, a master's of theological studies from the Washington Theological Union, and a doctorate in ministry from the Graduate Theological Foundation, Donaldson, Indiana. An educator at all levels from kindergarten through high school, she has spent the last fourteen years in pastoral ministry in a military chapel where she was active in liturgical ministry, hospital ministry, and adult spiritual programs. She now lives on Chincoteague Island, Virginia. With Bridget Mary Meehan she has coauthored *Heart Talks with Mother God* and *Affirmations from the Heart of God*.

Bridget Mary Meehan, SFCC, holds a doctorate in ministry from Virginia Theological Seminary. She is a spiritual director, conference speaker, consultant in women's spirituality and author of more than sixteen books including *The Healing Power of Prayer*, *Affirmations from the Heart of God*, *Praying with Women of the Bible*, *Walking the Prophetic Journey* (with Mary Beben), *Exploring the Feminine Face of God*, *Delighting in the Feminine Divine*, and *Heart Talks with Mother God*. Dr. Meehan offers a visionary approach to wholeness and healing for women and men as disciples of Jesus and equals in the contemporary world. She is also the producer and host of *Godtalk*, a new cable TV program that aims to nurture the soul, heal the heart, expand consciousness, transform lives, and inspire believers of all faiths.